Bible Legacy of the

BLACK RACE

The Prophecy Fulfilled

Joyce Andrews

Published and Distributed by:
Lushena Books
1804-06 West Irving Park Road
Chicago, IL 60613

ISBN 1-930097-18-2

Bible Legacy of the Black Race
The Prophecy Fulfilled

Joyce Andrews

Printed: July, 2000

Published and Distributed by:
Lushena Books, Inc.
1804 West Irving Park Road
Chicago, IL 60613

Library of Congress Catalog Card No: 92-85408
ISBN: 1-930097-18-2

Printed in the United States of America

To *my husband,*
Pastor Ben E. Andrews, for encouragement and tolerance when
supper was not ready on time.

To my sister,
Minnie Johnson, who was my late-night company-keeper.

To my daughter,
Jocelyn Anne Andrews, who was my best critic.

To my daughters,
Dana Marie and Denae Antoinette Andrews

To my son,
Cousy James Andrews

and a note of Appreciation
to my brother,
Randolph Johnson Jr. for his encouraging enthusiasm and support.

Acknowledgement

To the Holy Bible Faith Center Church Family, 1178 Avenue A,
Beaumont, Texas, for their prayers and support of this work from
the beginning. Many thanks to Yolanda Gail Duriso for her
encouragement and loyal support.

Publisher's Note

The plight of the black race since the fifteenth century has engendered a thriving reserve of news and interest for historians, cartographers, and other keepers of world records of knowledge. During the course of the European slave trade, the true and real facts about Africa (the land of Ham, Egypt, Akebu-Lan, Nubia, Kemet, or Ethiopia) were forgotten, and if not lost or destroyed, were placed in dungeons along with original Christian icons and left there as if they never existed. The black race became a fabulous phenomena of a curse, and earlier information and events apropos Africa became legends and myths. This modification of African history was one chief method the West had of fostering the formation of the European slave era. The new and transposed concepts of Africa condoned and softened the justification for trafficking human cargo.

"Whatever is done to them is better than what they are accustomed to" was one thought that found its way into European thinking during the fifteenth century, thus making the grand holocaust appear as a blessing in disguise. The Western countries were made to feel even more at ease when the Roman Catholic Bishop Bartalome de las Casas wrote his treatise as to why the Blacks of Africa were more suitable to be enslaved than the indigenous indian population. Crystalizing this treatise was the decree by Pope Julius II of Rome who gave carte blanche sanction that the Africans did not have souls and therefore bringing them from their heathenish lifestyle was not an ill act before God. Henceforth, the black race became a product for mass marketing.

The African slave involvement is the primary reason why Christianity in slave holding countries was never spiritually intended for the Black race in regard to Salvation, but as a means to oppression and confinement to a life of servanthood. The Holy scriptures were taught from a different perspective to the slaves who were compelled to attend these services held for them on the plantations. Further adding to the detriment of the slaves was the revision of the Bishop's Bible, now known as the Authorized King James Version. This allowed anyone to become an authority as to what to teach the African slaves. Biblical Ham became cursed and the black race became his accursed children. The Western church produced preachers who designed special sermons and teachings for Blacks with the usual themes of damnation for disobedience to the slave holders. The once proud Africans gave their bodies as ransom to the New World Order and their only purpose was not to serve God, but to serve the white race and whatever abomination fell upon the slave was justified by God himself.

But was this the plan of God? Could something as heinous as the European Slave trade, lasting for more than 400 years have gone unnoticed by a God of supreme love for all humankind?

The prophecy of God and the black race is what this book is about. Never before in biblical research has there been an interpretive understanding of prophesy concerning the black race as Joyce Andrews has outlined in *Bible Legacy of the Black Race, the Prophecy Fulfilled.* She makes it clear that there is a direct relationship between the present-day African diaspora and the ancient Egyptians. In ancient biblical times all Africans were referred to either as Ethiopians or Egyptians, Nubians and Lybians. Historical and archeaological facts have revealed much, but nothing to the extent of what is written in the Holy Bible. Three major biblical prophets of the Old Testament, Isaiah, Jeremiah and Ezekiel, spoke of the destiny of the black race relative to the disobedient and rebellious spirit the Egyptians had for the statutes, laws and commandments of God: The current plight of the black race is not entirely a result of Western caucasoid exploitation (although the latter was used as an instrument to carry out the plan of God). The eventful circumstances of the black race began with the utterance of the prophet Isaiah in the 19th and 20th chapters and from that point a series of prophecies and events unfolded that have effected the black race unto the fulfillment of the gentiles.

JAMES PEEBLES, PH.D.
PUBLISHER

Introduction

Several books and many articles have been written from a secular point of view, in an effort to explain the state of the Black race as it is today. Slavery has usually been given as the basic reason for its condition, but slavery was simply the consequential end result of a chain of events that took place over the many centuries from the time that black people ruled over nations.

Many people of practically all races, including some blacks, have the mistaken notion that the Black race's roots began in the bush of Africa and merely progressed through slavery and civil rights. Actually, the drama of blacks had its beginning in the Garden of Eden (this shall be discussed later in the book) moving onward in time to the great empires of the Pharaohs of Ancient Egypt, through the rise and fall of these great empires and ending in the bush and finally slavery.

African black people have long been regarded as among the most primitive people on the face of the earth. Although many tribal customs are slowly dying out as the people become more acquainted with the outside world, nevertheless, the majority of Africa's black people are basically illiterate. Evolutionists have often identified them as primitives who have yet to make the long climb upward toward civilization, believing that their environment, such as the bush, or some other misfortune may have held these people back, preventing any further advancement. However, historical and archaeological evidence support a different view. Through these findings it has been established, beyond doubt, that black people of African descent are the direct descendants of the Ancient Egyptians of Africa. These are the same Egyptians that are prominently mentioned in the Bible!

When Africa is mentioned in Scripture it is usually referred to as "The Land of Egypt". The name 'Egypt' is of uncertain origin but it is popularly believed to mean 'black', and Ethiopia is a Greek term meaning "burnt-faced". The African ancestors of black people were actually the very same Blacks that started civilization in the river valleys of Africa and Asia along the banks of the Nile River thousands of years before the era of the Pharaohs. Although it is disputed whether Egypt was the cradle of civilization, it is commonly agreed, according to Paul Johnson (*The Civilization Of Ancient Egypt*) that "it was the first to emerge as a national, as opposed to a city, culture. Egypt was not only the first state, it was the first country: it was the product not only of human ingenuity but of racial grouping and, above all, of a (very well-suited) geography". They were known and honored throughout the Ancient World for their architectural and engineering skills (the Egyptian pyramids are proof of that) and their unusual wisdom and knowledge. History reports they were a strong and powerful people with mighty armies and for thousands of years they ruled over other nations. Even today scientists stand in awe and amazement at their accomplishments and have found that they were also a very rich and prosperous people, as evidenced by the various tombs that have been uncovered in recent years of some of the kings and Pharaohs, such as King Tutankhamen and others.

Apparently, the American and African people are not primitives who are on their way up. Instead, they are a people whose ancestors had once reached the pinnacle of colossal success and then blew it and fell a long way down.

Scientists are still uncovering the evidence of this once-great Egyptian civilization that later fell into the ruins that it is today. Africa is often referred to as the "Dark Continent" or "Darkest Africa". The nation that once ruled over other nations and the builders of 'The Great Pyramids' is today regarded as primitive and the most backward of all the nations. Why? What happened to Egypt's great empire? How did it happen? From the exalted glory of Pharaohs, Kings and Queens to the lowly status of bush primitives and the shame of slavery. Why?

It must be remembered that the Bible, in addition to being a book based on spiritual matters, is also a history book. Of all books that have been written concerning the history of the Ancient Egyptians, none has ever approached the subject from a biblical point of view. Many were the reminiscences in days gone by of dear old great-great-great grandmothers who used to whisper softly and longingly to their children and grandchildren, "We's in the Bible". Being unable to read and write, they could never quote the book, chapter and verse but they knew for certain it was " . . . somewhere back in the Old Testament." Something in their spirits never quite forgot who they really were.

"Righteousness exalteth a nation: but sin is a reproach to any people." (Proverbs 14:34). It is common knowledge among Egyptologists, from their many archaeological discoveries and studies, that the Egyptians were a very religious people who, unfortunately, were deep into idol worship, sorcery and Satanism. The many temples and monuments, statues and long avenues of sphinxes that the world stand in awe and wonder over today, were actually the hundreds of pagan gods the Egyptians worshiped. The walls inside the many pyramids and tombs bear drawings testifying to their deep-rooted belief in sorcery and witchcraft. The famous sign of the serpent erected in the middle of the forehead of each Pharaoh's headdress is indicative of the satanic power that was so prevalent among Egyptians. Even some of the pottery that has been uncovered by archaeologists, bear the symbolic satanic sign of the goat's head. They worshiped the ram, the hawk, the lion, even statues that were part human and part beast.

It is supposed that many things may have contributed to the downfall of this great civilization, such as widespread epidemics, changes in trade routes, earthquakes, famines or any number of circumstances. But were they the *primary* cause? The Bible, as well as secular history, reveals explicitly why this great nation failed and is no longer in existence today. Nations and civilizations shall always fail when the people turn away from God and His laws. They cannot build or even sustain their empires without Him.

If we could mention, for example, a few other nations:

Babylon—Credited for the potter's wheel, the vault, the dome and the arch.

Phonecia—a nation of commerce that developed the English alphabet.

Greece—the first practicing of democracy, home of Socrates, Plato, and Aristotle.

Rome—The mighty conquerer and her great army.

History has revealed that moral and spiritual decay was at the heart of their decline.

It's interesting to note that black people are not the only descendants of ancestors who were once great and powerful. Beneath the dense bush foliage in Central America lies what remains of the once-great Mayan civilization. Scientists and historians have known for years that the Mayas were superb architects and accomplished astronomers and mathematicians. The Mayas developed the *positional system*, without which we would have no computers today. When the Phoenicians brought the concept of the zero into Europe from the Hindus, the Mayas had already been using it for at least a thousand years! These people even developed a network of drainage and irrigation canals, a complicated system that no doubt required great technological knowledge to design and build.

But eventually, disaster struck. In 1527 a handful of Spaniards rode in to begin the conquest of the Mayas and found the ancient cities already in ruins and the culture in decline. What had happened to the Mayas? Researchers believe that human sacrifices to the Pagan gods became more common toward the end of the Mayan era and that tens of thousands of people were slaughtered. The Spaniards rode in and conquered an already disintegrated society.

Whatever happened to the Mayan people after the fall of their great civilization? Recently, in the bush of southern Mexico, near the Guatemalan border, a tribe known as the Lacandones, a people regarded as among the most primitive people in the world, were discovered by scientists uncovering evidence of once-great civilizations that later fell into ruin. Presuming these people had never been civilized, they began to study them—their customs and language, their physical characteristics and general background and found, to their surprise and amazement, that the Lacandones are the direct descendants of the once-great and glorious Mayas! The Lacandones were not a primitive people on their way up, they were instead, a once great people who have come a long way down.

Another great people, familiar to most people and often mentioned in school textbooks, are the Incas. The famous *Royal Road* of the Incas was 3250 miles long, a distance greater than that from Los Angeles to Boston! The Incas built their cities entirely of stone and with such precision that mortar was unnecessary. Excavators have found an extravagant water system that has remained intact for centuries. Even more amazing evidence revealed that the Incas successfully performed brain surgery long before the time of Christ! But the mighty Inca civilization also crumbled from corruption within and collapsed in the 1500s.

Whatever became of these great people? In South America, near the Peruvian Andes just below the mountain tops, scientists have found another group of so-called "primitives" the Quechuas. There are some five million Quechuas, many of whom are addicted to cocaine. The average one has little desire to do anything but remain numb, anesthetized to life. Who are these so-called "primitive" people? They are the descendants of a people who established an empire that was to become a legend—the Incas!

The rise and fall of these two great civilizations were no different from the rise and fall of Ancient Egypt—moral decadence was the reason for the decline of them all. However, the most intriguing and astounding phenomenon concerning Ancient Egypt is the fact that the Bible records that before total destruction came upon Egypt, God sent prophets to warn the Pharaohs and all the land of

Egypt and Ethiopia. Over a period of 127 years God sent prophets to warn of the coming disaster that He had determined against the land of Egypt and Ethiopia.

About the year 714 B.C. God sent the first prophet, Isaiah, to warn Pharaoh and the Egyptians to forsake the worship of idols and the practice of sorcery. He was commanded to prophesy, not only against the people themselves, but also against the *land* as well, thereby changing the destiny of the entire nation and continent of Africa! Pharaoh did not heed the prophet's warning and, as a result, God allowed the prophecy to fall on the Egyptian nation, known today as Africa, and upon all of Egypt's descendants as well (present-day blacks of African descent) thereby effecting changes and transformations that have plagued the lives of black people even to this very day!

Studying the prophecy that God gave to the prophet Isaiah, it becomes apparent how the consequences of the prophecy, once it began to go into execution, fell on all the Egyptians and their descendants, commencing a change in the very nature of the Egyptian. These changes that Isaiah prophesied against the people and against the land, have through the centuries, steadfastly conformed to every phase of the prophecy, resulting in characteristics and traits that are prevalent in most black people all over the world.

In studying the fulfillment of the prophecy and its various aspects, the obvious traits, singularities and peculiarities that have always earmarked the behavioral pattern of black people, will become clear and apparent. For instance, the black-on-black violence that prevails among blacks is a result of the fulfillment of the prophecy against the Egyptians and their descendants. Also the peculiar and unreasonable dislike that black people generally have toward one another and the inability to come together and work together as one, plus the consistent high rate of unemployment that has always been the black race's lot, just to name a few. All these, and much more, were prophesied against the Ancient

Egyptians and were allowed to follow their descendants (black people of African descent) throughout the ensuing centuries, up to this present day! Also, the portion of prophecy that was prophesied against the land has, through the centuries, effected many changes on the continent of Africa, such as heavy drought, famine, jungles, deserts and the like. God warned Egypt that all these things would come to pass if they did not heed. However, it is also important to bear in mind that Isaiah foretold that one day there would be an end (fulfillment) of the prophecy and a restoration of black people.

As the prophecies that God gave the prophets Isaiah, Jeremiah and Ezekiel are studied, questions that have plagued the hearts of black people for hundreds of years will become better understood.

The mighty Egypt, land of the Pharaohs, Kings and Queens, was the world's first centralized government. Scientists are still uncovering ancient relics of this great civilization in an effort to discover its age-old secrets and to possibly discover why it finally collapsed after reigning as a world power for over three thousand years.

The rise and fall of this once mighty civilization is of particular interest because these Ancient Egyptians are the ancestors of black people of African descent. The prophecy God gave to Isaiah the prophet regarding Egypt was intended, in the beginning, to describe the calamities that *could* come upon Egypt and the effect that they *could* have upon the people and the land itself if the nation did not repent of its idolatry and sorcery. The warning was intended to produce an alarm among the people of the nation so great that the consequences of disobedience would certainly turn them from sorcery and idol-worship and they would seek to the one God Jehovah. However, the warning predicting the downfall of Pharaoh and the desolation of the land of Egypt went totally unheeded by the Egyptians and consequently, the prophecy came to pass and fell on the Egyptians and their descendants (black people of African descent), the consequences of which are yet prevalent among black people, even to this present day!

As we look into some of the leading events in the history of Egypt (Africa) we can more clearly determine the application of the different parts of the prophecy against the Egyptians and the land of Egypt.

At the height of its power, about 1560 B.C., the Egyptian empire had spread beyond the Nile Valley to Palestine and Syria. The nations that acknowledged Egypt's supremacy routinely sent quantities of ivory, gold and spices to its temples and courts. In 1240 B.C., following the reign of the last great Pharaoh, Ramses II, who is thought to be the Pharaoh who oppressed the Israelites, Egypt began to slowly decline. Pharaoh-Necho, in 608 B.C., won a notable victory in Palestine over Josiah's army. However, about three years later, history (and the Bible) records that Necho was severely defeated in battle by Nebuchadnezzar of Babylonia.

As the prophecy of Isaiah unfolds, the defeat of Pharaoh-Necho by Nebuchadnezzar simply marked the beginning of the fulfillment of the prophecy and the end of Egyptian civilization as it had formerly been. Apries, a later Pharaoh of the dynasty, was deposed about 569 B.C. by Ahmose II. In 525 B.C., however, his son and successor, Psammetichus III was conquered by Cambyses II, king of Persia, bringing to a close more than 3,000 years of almost continuous Egyptian rule, culture and independence. With the defeat of Psammetichus III came the end of native Egyptian reign. Under Cambyses II, Egyptian rule gave way to Persian and Persian rule eventually gave way to Alexander the Great, who was followed by the Ptolemies who ruled Egypt for over two hundred years, who in turn, gave way to the Romans.

All that followed in the ensuing centuries may be viewed as a continuous fulfillment of God's decree. Minute detail of the fulfillment of the prophecy is boldly manifested, bearing itself out in history, for God sometimes fulfills His decree by a gradual process rather than an immediate one, with the hope that there will be repentance before His decree finally comes to fruition.

Chapter 1

"The burden of Egypt. Behold, the Lord rideth upon a swift cloud, and shall come into Egypt: and the idols of Egypt shall be moved at His presence, and the heart of Egypt shall melt in the midst of it."—Isaiah 19:1

The very first thing God did was to destroy the idols. Here lies the explanation of *why* the many great and exquisite temples, statues and monuments of Egypt are today only relics and wonders of the past. "Thou shalt have no other gods before me." The religious beliefs of the ancient Egyptians were the dominating influence of their entire culture, although true religion, in the sense of a unified worship of one god, never existed among them. For thousands of years the Egyptians had no well-defined religion. Their faith was a disorganized collection of ancient myths, nature worship, and hundreds of

The Colossi of Memnon.
Ancient Thebes

deities and gods. The gods were represented with human bodies and animal heads or vice-versa. Out of the hundreds worshiped by the Egyptians, the only important god that was worshiped with any consistency was Amon-Ra and as their religion became more involved, deities were confused with humans who had been deified after death. During the 5th Dynasty (2494–2345 B.C.) the Pharaohs themselves began to claim divine ancestry and from that time on were worshiped as sons of Amon-Ra.

The Court of Rameses II within the ruins of Luxor Temple.

The world's oldest stone structures were built by the Ancient Egyptians and practically all of their well-known monuments and tombs are made of stone. The stone, to them, represented a substance that would last forever, hence their reason for limiting its use almost exclusively throughout Egyptian history to places for the dead, in tombs, and for their gods, in temples. Practically all of their great and outstanding works that have lasted through the centuries are based out of their belief in their gods and in life after death. In the book, *The Civilization of Ancient Egypt*, Paul Johnson states: "The Egyptians, having discovered eternity, associated it in their minds with their native hardstones, which seemed to last forever, and so prepared bodies for burial with stone implements and equipment."

The world-wide practice of embalming dead bodies originated with the Egyptians because they believed that the souls could not exist without the body therefore every effort was made to preserve the corpse by embalming and mummifying. So skilled were they in their craft that the soles of the feet of mummies, when unwrapped after as many as 3,000 years, were still soft and elastic. Therefore, as a final protection, elaborate tombs were erected to protect the corpse and other burial accompaniments.

These great tombs, pyramids as we know them, were famous throughout the ancient world and the Great Pyramid was one of the 'Seven Wonders' of the world. Amazingly, it stands today as the only remaining 'Wonder' left in existence. So accurately were they built, with the familiar perfect symmetrical form, that the base lacks but a fraction of an inch of being a perfect square! Such were the engineering skills of the early Egyptians. The Great Pyramid itself is large enough to contain St. Paul's Cathedral, Westminster Abbey, St. Peter's at Rome, and the Cathedrals of Florence and Milan!

The Great Sphinx, at the height of its fame, was the marvel of civilization. It is yet referred to as "The World's Most Wonderful Statue". Except for the paws, it is carved out of one block of stone. The grandest of the temples were the Temple of Amon-Ra and the Temple of Luxor. These were connected by a paved avenue seventy-six feet wide and a mile and a quarter long, known as the "Avenue of the Sphinxes". On either side were palms and beautiful gardens of flowers and shrubs, but the immediate border of the avenue was lined with almost one thousand human and ram-headed sphinxes—nearly five hundred on each side! The temple of Amon, or Karnak, was 338 feet wide and 1200 feet long—the largest ever reared by the hand of man. More than a hundred pyramids, in six groups, are clustered around Memphis, the capital of the Old Kingdom.

" . . . and the idols of Egypt shall be moved (destroyed) at his presence." Today these temples, pyramids and other fabulous structures of Egypt constitute the greatest and most extensive set of ruins known to man. History tells us that many of them were shattered by an earthquake. The only remains are granite blocks, broken obelisks. statues, and columned streets. For over 2,000 years they lay buried beneath ten to twenty feet of shifting sand until the latter part of the nineteenth century, when excavators were able to show its layout and to exhibit the many interesting objects discovered after having lain under the desert sands.

> "And I will set the Egyptians against the Egyptians: and they shall fight every one against his brother, and everyone against his neighbor, city against city, and kingdom against kingdom."— Isaiah 19:2

There were two main factors that contributed to the unity and togetherness that existed among the early Egyptians: (1) the geographical location of the Nile Valley which provided isolation from the rest of the world and (2) the fact that the superstitious Egyptians greatly feared leaving Egypt because they thought they would die in a foreign land and miss eternity. It is this inherent unity among the Egyptian people that God prophesies shall no longer exist among them. "And I will set the Egyptians against the Egyptians." This prophecy has followed Egyptian descendants through the centuries, for it is not customary for black people to cooperate and pull together on any one issue; usually there is a spirit of disunity. The fact that most black people generally seem to harbor an unexplainable dislike for each other, showing more of a spirit of goodwill towards people of another race than towards people of their own race is based in the fulfillment of this prophecy: "And I will set the Egyptians against the Egyptians . . ."

Scattered about in the bush and unable to come together

4

because of a spirit of disunity that existed among them, the Africans were easy pickings for the slave traders and other exploiters that descended upon the continent, and simply could not stand against them to prevent the kidnapping of so many millions. Although the conquering Europeans enjoyed the advantage of more superior weapons against the brave African warriors, armed only with spears and a lot of courage, the factor that really turned things in favor of the Europeans was *other Africans*. Without other Africans supplying soldiers, intelligence, carriers, food supplies, services and secret agents, the Europeans would never have been able to conquer the nation.

The concerted actions of the Berlin Conference of 1885, whose main purpose was to divide up the continent of Africa good and proper among themselves, was done against a divided and disconcerted people, unable to cooperate together to expel the foreigners out of their land as any other country would have done. Today, the problem that makes it difficult for the new nations of Africa to govern themselves successfully is a lack of unity among the people. In some of the countries, such as Nigeria, disunity between the tribes has led to tragic civil wars. Most Africans are still accustomed to thinking of themselves as members of a tribe rather than citizens of a country. Because of special tribal loyalties, they will generally vote for leaders who belong to their own tribe rather than work together for the common good. It is this characteristic among the Blacks that partly accounts for the control and rulership the white man exercises over the African people. The ability of 5 million whites in South Africa to rule over 28 million Blacks could not be were it not for the spirit of disunity that exists and the inability to come together as one nation. It is a situation that God allowed to be that His word might come to pass concerning what He had prophesied against the Egyptians and their descendants: "And I will set the Egyptians against the Egyptians . . ." God commanded the prophet to warn Pharaoh that the Egyptians, as a nation and as a people, would eventually come to

5

such a state if they continued in satanism (idolatry and sorcery).

"... and they shall fight every one against his brother ..."

Many black people have been killed at the hands of many white people, but more Blacks have been killed at the hands of their own black brothers and sisters than *by any other race*. Before the arrival of the Europeans, organized warfare among the African tribes flourished, with the chiefest and best-known among them being the Zulus. The most powerful figure among them was the Zulu, Shaka. In the book, *Discovery of Africa*, by Richard Hall, he quotes, "At the height of his power, Shaka was able to put 100,000 warriors in the field. His armies conquered and destroyed far and wide, absorbing all the Nguni groups. Shaka's cruelty was notorious; warriors were executed for the most trivial indiscipline. ... one group under Zwangendaba pillaged as far as Lake Victoria over several decades. Another, led by Mzilikazi, set up the Matabel Empire beyond the Limpopo River; a third, led by Sbetwane, conquered the Barotse Kingdom beyond the Zambezi.

Shaka was murdered by his half-brothers and one of these Dingane, took over from him. Under Dingane, the Zulu armies *depopulated* neighboring areas. They remained unbeaten until, under the reign of Cetewayo in the nineteenth century, they were confronted with White power. The rise and fall of the Zulus was to typify the limitations of Africa's warrior empire: without literacy it was impossible to maintain a stable administration and without firearms the onset of European rule could not be halted."

"... and they shall fight every one against his brother ..."

According to the 1989 World Almanac: "Ethnic or tribal clashes made Africa the chief world locus of sustained warfare in the late 1970's." Even at this very moment as I am relating these things (August 27, 1990), world headlines are screaming the violence taking place between African Blacks! Internal strife and deadly destructive warfare has been raging in the townships surrounding Johannesburg, between the Zulus and the Xhosas, Africa's two largest tribes and long-time rivals. Zulus, armed with

6

rifles, raided an Xhosa Workers barracks killing twenty-two people and pushing the death toll to 364 in a week of tribal clashes.

". . . and they shall fight every one against his brother . . ."

Is this characteristic peculiar only among Blacks in Africa? Sadly, no. Black-on-Black crime is a hard, unavoidable fact in America and black men are destroying themselves in record numbers, dying violent and needless deaths at each other's hands by the scores.

National statistics disclosed that in America, homicide is the leading cause of death for black men between the ages of fifteen and twenty-four. 51 percent of the violent crimes committed in the United States are by black youth. One out of every six black males will be arrested by the time he reaches nineteen years old. Moreover, one in every four black men between the ages of twenty

7

and twenty-nine years old is either in prison, on probation or on parole. Black-on-Black violence. How often has the question been asked, 'Why is this type of behavior—killing, stabbing, shooting—so characteristic of and so prevalent among black people?'

" . . . and they shall fight every one against his brother . . ."

According to a recent study, the nation's capital, Washington, D.C., whose population is 70 percent Black, is recorded as being the murder capital of the world.

" . . . and they shall fight every one against his brother . . ."

The prophecy, that went totally unheeded by Pharaoh and the Egyptians, was allowed to go into effect, and fell on the Egyptians and their descendants (black people of African descent).

" . . . and they shall fight every one against his neighbor . . ."

It was a common practice, during slavery, for one Black to inform against his other black brothers, in spite of the fact that they were all in the same 'boat'. One of the Belgian Congo's biggest hurdles on the path to organizing into a nation was the hostility that exists between many of the tribes. In 1957 the Belgian Congo government granted voting rights to the Africans and the right to form social and cultural societies. But, much faster than the authorities expected, the societies turned into political parties—sixty of them, all divided along tribal lines! Two of the Congo's eastern neighbors, the Kingdom of Burundi and the Republic of Rwanda, were also afflicted with tribal difficulties. There the Bahutu still bitterly remember their former subservience to the giant Watusi, whose men average six feet, six inches in height. This resentment was a major reason for the emergence of two nations rather than one, in July, 1962. Because of each one's resentment against his neighbor, consequently, the Bahutu is in charge of Rwanda and the Watusi is in charge of Burundi. " . . . and they shall fight every one against his neighbor . . ."

" . . . city against city, and kingdom against kingdom." In Africa, this could be translated 'tribe against tribe' or 'village against village'. In America it could be translated 'this gang against that gang' or 'this group against that group', especially if one group is trying to elevate itself to a higher educational or financial plane, giving some credence to the old saying concerning the crabs in the bucket. Whether *near* (city against city) or *far away* (kingdom against kingdom), wherever black people should congregate, in the bush or in the ghettoes, in the city or in the country, on the streets or in the nightclubs, these traits of typical behavior—fighting, arguing, murder, violence of every form—would most often occur.

Through the centuries, in Africa, tribes have been known to rise up against other tribes and practically wipe each other out because of frequent tribal feuds. Some villages, which usually consist of two long rows of huts facing each other, are built with the village's lower end opened onto the shore of the river and the upper end is closed to enable the villagers to defend themselves in case of attack by other tribes. The Bantu tribes generally live in a group of huts arranged in a circle which makes it easy to protect the settlement not only from wild animals but also from unfriendly tribes as well. " . . . city against city, kingdom against kingdom." The prophet warned Pharaoh and Egypt that if there was not a change in the hearts of the people to turn away from idolatry and sorcery, these things would surely come to pass.

> "And the spirit of Egypt shall fail in the midst thereof; and I shall destroy the counsel thereof: AND THEY SHALL SEEK TO THE IDOLS, AND TO THE CHARMERS, AND TO THEM THAT HAVE FAMILIAR SPIRITS, AND TO THE WIZARDS."— Isaiah 19:3

Egypt was not only recognized throughout the ancient world as a world power with great abilities, but also famous for its spiritual knowledge and counseling. However, the more the Egyptians turned to idolatry, the more their spiritual counsel became based in sorcery and witchcraft. Egyptians, in those days, were what is called today spiritualists, mediums and fortunetellers. It was for this reason that God would become so angry with the Israelites when they would often choose to go down into Egypt for counseling and advice, totally ignoring the counsel of God's prophets and displaying scorn and contempt for God's word.

> "Woe to the rebellious children, saith the Lord, that take counsel, but not of me . . .that walk to go down into Egypt, and have not asked at my mouth; to strengthen themselves in the strength of Pharaoh, and to trust in the shadow of Egypt. Therefore shall the strength of Pharaoh be your shame, and the trust in the shadow of Egypt your confusion. For his princes were at Zoan and his ambassadors came to Hanes . . .
> The burdens of the beasts of the south: into the land of trouble and anguish, from whence came the young and old lion, the viper and fiery flying serpent, they will carry their riches upon the shoulders of young asses, and their treasures upon the bunches of camels, to a people that shall not profit them, for the Egyptians shall help in vain, and to no purpose: Therefore have I cried concerning this, Their strength is to sit still." —Isaiah 30:1–7

" . . . and I shall destroy the *counsel* thereof . . ." God warns that He will destroy the validity of their famous wisdom and the spirit of pride that the Egyptians had over the fact that other nations sought them for counsel, direction, guidance and instruction. This outstanding ability also contributed to the great fame of Egypt. So accurate was their counsel that the Israelites would, at much hazard and danger to themselves (young and old lions, vipers, and fiery flying serpents) travel to Egypt (walk) to strengthen themselves in the strength of Pharaoh, and to trust in the shadow of Egypt.

" . . . The burden of the beasts of the south . . ." This expression referred to the common sight of the caravans and beasts of burdens (the young asses and bunches of camels) that were laden down with heavy loads of rich treasure, traveling southward towards Egypt, even as far away as Zoan and Hanes. It was customary then, even as it is today, to bring a present, gift of money, or other valuables, when consulting with spiritualists, fortunetellers, palm readers and the like.

" . . . they will carry their riches upon the shoulders of young asses, and their treasures upon the bunches of camels, to a people that shall not profit them. For the Egyptians shall help in vain, and to no purpose: therefore have I cried concerning this . . ."

At this point, it should be understood that the Jews and other nations were not seeking out the Egyptians solely for their fortunetellers, spiritualists and mediums. Much of their confidence in the Egyptians was centered around the fact that the Egyptians excelled in practically every field of endeavor known to the ancient world at that time, including architecture, sculpture, painting, navigation, medicine, the industrial arts and sciences and astronomy. In the field of science, for example, the Egyptians displayed a remarkable knowledge of physiology, surgery, the circulatory system of the blood, and the science of asepsis (special methods used to prevent infection). Therefore, it is possible that the Jews and other nations also availed themselves of the Egyptians' knowledge of surgeries, medicines and how to treat certain ailments of the body. The modern-day phrase would be, "They were placing more faith in Egyptians than they were in God". It's also possible that Moses was not the only Jew educated in Egypt because mathematics was a formal study in Egypt as early as 2900 B.C.

There was much wisdom to be learned from the Egyptians. Acts 7:22 reveals that ". . . Moses was learned in all the wisdom of the Egyptians, and was mighty in words and in deeds." Egypt's fame for wisdom was second only to King Solomon himself! 1 Kings 4:30—"And Solomon's wisdom excelled the wisdom of all the children of the east country, and all the wisdom of Egypt." No

11

other nation or kingdom was as renowned for great wisdom and knowledge as was Egypt.

But God decreed: ". . . I will *destroy* the *counsel* thereof; and they shall seek to the idols, and to the charmers, and to them that have familiar spirits, and to the wizards." God warns that their spirit of counsel would fail, and He would destroy the accuracy, the validity of their wisdom and would cause them to rely on the deceptive and deluding practice of sorcery and witchcraft. "They shall seek to the idols . . . charmers . . . familiar spirits . . . wizards." As this portion was eventually fulfilled, sorcery and witchcraft became even more prevalent among black people. Because witchcraft was nearly always practiced among black people, it became known as *black magic*.

The practice of voodoo and hoodoo came to America from Africa, brought over by the slaves on slave ships. Not only is it practiced in America, but also in the African diaspora: Haiti, Central America, the Caribbean, Brazil, Panama, and others. In fact, this practice is still very much alive among many American Blacks today. As a child, growing up in the South, it was common to know a fortuneteller or someone who could 'read the cards, palms, and tea leaves.' Someone who was known to be a witch or a warlock or had some type of familiar spirit could always be found somewhere in the neighborhood. I remember my mother used to "read the cards" for some people in the neighborhood and I can yet remember my surprise over the fact that most of her clientele were supposedly "church folk". And for reasons I didn't understand at the time, the practice was always found among black people. Why? Because the prophet Isaiah warned Pharaoh and all of Egypt that if they did not repent of sorcery and idolatry, the Egyptians and their descendants would be given over entirely to sorcery and its consequences. "They would seek to the *idols* (voodoo dolls, talismans and necklaces, amulets, candlesticks), *Charmers* (people who cast spells), *familiar spirits* (mediums, spiritualists, fortunetellers), *Wizards* (witches, warlocks, witch doctors, medicine men).

A wallpainting from one of the tombs at Thebes.

It is imperative, at this point, to know that the Egyptians were deep into the practice of sorcery, and had been for hundreds of years. As a matter of fact, we can estimate just how deeply into sorcery they really were by the contest between Moses and Pharaoh's magicians and sorcerers after God had commanded Pharaoh to let the children of Israel go. When Aaron cast down his rod before Pharaoh and it became a serpent, "Then Pharaoh also called the wise men and the sorcerers: now the magicians of Egypt, they also did in like manner with their enchantments." (Exodus 7:10–11).

". . . And he (Aaron) lifted up the rod, and smote the waters that were in the river, in the sight of Pharaoh, and in the sight of his servants; and all the waters that were in the river were turned to blood. And the magicians of Egypt did so with their enchantments." (Exodus 7:20–22). Exodus 8:6–8 also relates: "And Aaron stretched out his hand over the waters of Egypt; and the frogs came up, and covered the land of Egypt. And the magicians did so with their enchantments, and brought up frogs upon the land of Egypt." Using the powers of sorcery, the Egyptians were able to duplicate some of the very superfeats that God Himself was able to do, proving how deep into sorcery they really were! Nowhere else in the Bible is it recorded of any other nation of people who could perform such acts of that nature except the Ancient Egyptians. Therefore, as they had fallen down so deeply into the pits of satanism, God deemed it necessary to issue a final warning.

Pharaoh, however, did not heed the prophet's warning and consequently, the prophecy was fulfilled in the lives of the Egyptians and their descendants. God decreed that since they preferred to make satanic spirits their source of wisdom and power, He would give them over entirely to the practice of sorcery and witchcraft ". . . even as they did not like to retain God in their knowledge, God gave them over to a reprobate mind, to do those things which are not convenient." (Romans 1:28).

It is for this reason that in Africa today, the *witch doctor* exercises such power and influence among the African people. Many missionaries have confirmed that their biggest hindrance in converting the African people to Christianity is the power of the people's belief in the *witch doctor*. Although many people of Africa have been converted to Christianity, there are the majority who remain indigenous to their beliefs, indulging in the worship of spirits, a practice kept alive and well by the *witch doctor* or so-called *medicine man*. It is a known fact that the *medicine man* is the priest of the African villages and the people fear him greatly because they believe that he has power to command the spirits. He sells them charms to protect them from wild beasts, sickness, evil men and the selfsame evil spirits. The people also believe that he can bring dreadful diseases upon the village or cause a man to die. He is usually a very cunning person, able to mix up powerful poisons and capitalize on the fears of the people.

> "There shall not be found among you *any one* that useth divination (divining rods), or an observer of times (astrology, horoscopes, omens) or an enchanter (a person who uses words to call up the devil), or a witch (someone who practices witchcraft), or a charmer (casts spells), or a consulter with familiar spirits (mediums, fortunetellers) or a wizard (warlock, witch doctor, medicine man), or a necromancer (spiritualists who call up the dead).—Deuteronomy 18:10–11

> "And the Egyptians will I give over into the hand of a cruel lord; and a fierce king shall rule over them, saith the Lord, the Lord of hosts."—Isaiah 19:4

This is the first mention of slavery to Pharaoh and the Egyptians. Isaiah prophesies hard bondage for the Egyptians under the hand of a cruel lord (slavemasters) and fierce, unmerciful rulers and kings. History bears out the fulfillment of this prophecy. It is reported by some sources that the European slave trade began as early as 1444 and continued for more than four hundred years. However, it is commonly believed that around 1498 Portuguese navigators, trying to find a route around Africa, became acquainted with its West coast regions and established settlements there. There they also saw natives wearing gold ornaments. *Gold!* In spite of the heat, humidity and mosquitoes, they returned again and again to obtain the precious metal and soon were bringing back slaves as well as gold. The knowledge of the wealth to be obtained in the region soon attracted explorers, traders and colonizers from England, Spain, Holland, France and Denmark. Before long, the European shipmasters visited the coast to primarily carry off slaves. The slave trade proved especially profitable for these and other nations and during the next four centuries an estimated 100 million Africans were seized and transported into slavery.

"And the Egyptians will I give over into the hand of a cruel lord." The height of cruelty in the American slavery system was, above all the other cruelties, the exploitation of the minds of the African people, a fact that stands out—to surpass the suffering and exploitation of any other race, bar none. Slavemasters, with few exceptions, recognized the necessity of mind control and began an assault on the minds of slaves that was of unparalleled severity. Power alone was not enough. A slave had to be made to believe himself, that he was a slave. Through various methods, each slave was taught that he or she was inferior, totally helpless and to always stand in awe of the white man's power. He was to obey every white man (no matter how mean, low or poor), on first command, without questioning or thinking. These lessons, which were well taught through many means and methods, were well learned. Traces of this mentality do yet remain in segments of the black community even to this day, although much of it has been eradicated.

". . . And a fierce king shall rule over them, saith the Lord, the Lord of hosts." For over three hundred years, from the beginning of the 16th century to the last quarter of the 19th century, Africa was explored and colonized. However, the Royal British Empire of Great Britain in England remained the principle ruling and governing power in Africa.

In July 1885, the Belgian Congo was placed under the personal sovereign rule of King Leopold II of Belgium. Leopold reigned over a portion of Africa that was as large as the 13 colonies put together, and with this reign came a new form of terror. Harsh methods were marked by the existence of widespread, horrifying atrocities that were done against the Africans. Natives that did not produce as much as was expected were often mutilated, having one of their limbs, a hand, foot or fingers chopped off and used as an example for the other workers. Whole villages were burned down and a child would be killed for the offense of the parents. The native Africans, content to simply work their own land, were not interested in working the plantations and mills for the white man. Therefore, the establishment of taxes in most of the colonies were payable only in cash, forcing the people to have to grow cash crops or sell their labors. Forced labor imposed upon the natives was so severe and natives of the Congo were so ill-treated that international protests against these conditions finally forced the Belgian Parliament to adopt, on August 20, 1908, a treaty of cession against Leopold and his company.

> "And the waters shall fail from the sea, and the river shall be wasted and dried up. And they shall turn the rivers far away; and the brooks of defense shall be emptied and dried up: the reeds and flags shall wither.
> The paper reeds by the brooks, by the mouth of the brooks, and everything sown by the brooks, shall wither, be driven away, and be no more. The fishers also shall mourn, and all they that cast angle into the brooks shall lament, and they that spread nets upon the waters shall languish."—Isaiah 19:5–8

This portion of prophecy explains the reason behind the severe drought condition that exists in Africa today. It's no accident, fluke, or chance happening. Nothing happens without God's foreknowledge of it, and if He is forced to bring judgement upon sin, He always gives a more than sufficient warning first. "And the waters shall fail from the sea, and the river shall be wasted and dried up." Over one third of the continent of Africa is desert wasteland. The Sahara Desert, located in Africa, is the largest desert in the world and one of the most barren and desolate areas on earth. At present, it occupies approximately 3,500,000 square miles, an area as large as the United States! In addition to the Namib Desert, Arabian Desert, Libyan Desert and Nubian Desert, besides the Eastern and Western deserts, there is also the Kalahari Desert, which is reported to have once been the home of vast herds of game, but is now a useless wasteland.

For reasons known only to God, the Sahara, which stretches across North Africa from the Atlantic Ocean to the Red Sea, was already desert land during the time of the Ancient Egyptians. The valley of the Nile is, geographically, a part of the Sahara but the presence of the Nile River flowing through, transforms it into fertile agricultural land throughout much of Egypt. From about 2000 B.C. the Sahara, as well as its eastern extension across Egypt and the Sinai peninsula area had begun to lose rainfall and dry up. However, it was not the advanced case of desiccation that it is today. Some of the rock paintings, discovered by archaeologists, depict horse-drawn chariots in the Sahara. This mode of transportation was used in the Sahara as late as 500 B.C. As desert conditions continued to gradually expand, chariots were replaced by the camel, which to this day is yet a familiar sight navigating their way across the hot, dusty sands using certain wind patterns, stars and the sun as a guide. Because it has the highest evaporation rates in the world, it is continuing to dry up. It contains the largest areas on the face of the earth that receives no precipitation for years at a time, and according to scientists' reports, is continuing to expand at the rate of 45 miles a year! The 1983 Encyclopedia Britannica states: "The earth's largest desert, the Sahara, remains to this day, a challenge to the mind of men. Proposals to alter natural conditions on a large scale have often been made . . . but the resultant climactic benefits are doubtful. The basic causes of Saharan aridity are climactic and far beyond man's power to alter."

Drought conditions in the northern Ethiopian province of Eritrea have prevented proper cultivation of fields, resulting in an 80 percent crop loss. What little soil that is available for growing food is depleted of nutrients; the dry dusty, barren fields cannot produce life-sustaining grains. Tens of thousands of children, many of them abandoned or orphaned, are threatened with starvation. Experts predict that within the next few years, northern Ethiopia may experience still another major famine. "And the brooks of defence shall be emptied and dried up: the reeds and flags shall wither. The paper reeds by the brooks, by the mouth of the brooks, and everything sown by the brooks, shall wither, be driven away and be no more."

"Moreover they that work in fine flax, and they that weave networks, shall be confounded."—Isaiah 19:9

Fine flax is fine linen and Egypt produced the best flax and turned out the best linen of its day. Renown for their fine linen weaving, the beautiful royal robes worn by the great Pharaohs and their Queens practically dominated the fashion scene of that day. These same fashions were still worn 2,600 years later by the famous and notorious Queen Cleopatra who, according to legend, was a light brown-skinned woman but in reality, was of Macedonian descent and had no Egyptian blood. The movie of the famous Queen used copies of the original gowns, jewelry and other attire that the real Cleopatra wore. The artistic designs, colors and lovely styles the Egyptians originated were superior to all others and are still dominant in some of the formal fashions of today. This fact explains why black people are inherently inclined to dress up and wear beautiful clothes (the lovely colors and styles of African costumes attest to this). White people prefer the casual look in clothing but black people have always loved beautiful and colorful (not to say 'loud') clothes and elaborate jewelry, a trait inherent, passed down from Ancient Egyptian ancestors.

Even the bed linens that came from Egypt were considered the

19

very finest in the world. In Proverbs 7:16 the harlot uses, as one of her enticing tools, the fact that she decks her bed with fine linen made in Egypt. "I have decked my bed with coverings of tapestry, with carved works, *with fine linen of Egypt.*"

Egypt is said to be the first country in history to develop a great artistic culture. According to Paul Johnson: "Egypt was the first civilization to emerge as a national as opposed to a city culture." The arts and crafts of the Nile Valley dominated the art world for more than 2,000 years, from about 2900 B.C. to about 600 B.C. when cultural dominance passed to the Greeks. Therefore, when the prophet declared that ". . . they that work in fine flax . . . and . . . weave networks, shall be confounded", he was warning Pharaoh that one day Egypt would no longer be recognized for excelling in the finer skills, their abilities would be 'confounded' or confused. The literal meaning, according to *Vine's Expository Dictionary of Old and New Testament Words*, is 'to put to shame'. ". . . and they that weave networks . . ." referred to those who were skilled in weaving the beautiful networks of fine embroidery and the elaborate embellishments that usually adorned Egyptian apparel. In other words, Egypt, as a race and a nation, would no longer be honored or widely acclaimed for their ability to excel in the finer arts. This declaration, without doubt, establishes the undeniable fact of the omnipotence and omniscience of Almighty God. Only an all-powerful God could declare over a nation that He was about to 'withdraw' His bounty of natural expertise, mastery of skills, and other outstanding knowhow abilities that this nation, over the centuries, had taken for granted, presuming them to be just a naturally occurring phenomenon that would always be, regardless. When a nation has been blessed to excel above other nations, it is not because of their natural human abilities but the grace and favor of God. However, when a nation turns from God and loses that favor, their abilities and powers will soon began to diminish.

Because of this prophecy, black people as a nation were never

again the recipients of special recognition and acclaim in the areas of fine arts and skills. The abilities were there but God chose to minimize them. Many inventions widely used, even up to this day, will never be identified with their black inventors because black people, especially during slavery, were not allowed to receive credit for their accomplishments. Usually their masters were given the credit for their inventions. Necessity, which often inspires invention, was the stimulus for Blacks who invented common everyday items as the alarm clock, the mop and the ironing board, the lawn mower, the pencil sharpener and the egg beater. Even the 3-color stoplight was invented by a Black as was potato chips and the gas mask that firemen use today. The black man who invented the golf ball tee used to have to hold the ball in place while the golfer swung. Dr. Vera Williams, a Black retired elementary school principal reports, "That brother got tired of getting his hand hit." The beautiful and popular hymn, *Precious Lord, Take my Hand*, was written by Thomas Dorsey who wrote many other hymns and songs that have graced the hymn books of American churches for many years but few people know that he was a black man. It is only in recent years that black people have begun to excel above singing, dancing, boxing and running track.

> "And they shall be broken in the purposes thereof, all that make sluices and ponds for fish."—Isaiah 19:10

The Egyptians also excelled in jewelry-making and all their jewelry was made from pure gold because gold was and still is plentiful in Africa. A *sluice* was a structure with a gate that controlled the flow of water and was used by the Egyptians to wash gold from sand and gravel. Jewelry-making, because of its important role in Egyptian costumes and burial clothes, was a highly developed skill among them and a very important livelihood. The craftsmen of Ancient Egypt produced exceptionally fine creations: lavishly intricate collar necklaces, bracelets, clasps and pectorals that were often worn on the chest. Their works were simply superb and were usually made of fine gold and inlaid with semi-precious stones. Egyptian jewelry and metal works are still considered the most beautiful ever produced, and European goldsmiths have rarely surpassed their works. The use of gold was extremely lavish; palace furniture and chariots were heavily encrusted with the precious metal. Royal seals, that were made of stone, pottery or crystal, were often set in rings or mountings of solid gold.

Paul Johnson quotes from his book: ". . . they did manufacture and wear large quantities of fine jewelry rings, diadems, earrings, anklets, bangles, and girdles, featuring gold, silver and electrum, and felspar, cornelian, amethst, jasper, lapiz-lazuli, garnets and haematite."

And they shall be broken in the purposes thereof, all that make sluices *and ponds for fish*." The *sluices* were associated with those who worked with gold and jewelry, a position that carried with it a degree of prestige. They that make *ponds for fish* was in reference to the average unskilled worker. This proclamation leaves no doubt as to who's in charge when it comes to national greatness and power. ". . . The Lord maketh poor, and maketh rich: He bringeth low, and lifteth up." (1 Samuel 2:6–7). Although Pharaoh could not perceive of it at the time, God was warning that the great accomplishments that Egypt was widely acclaimed for as a nation and as a people would no longer continue to be. This was also a real threat to the prestige of Egypt. "And they shall be *broken in the purposes thereof* . . ." According to *Vine's*, the word *purpose* used in the possessive case translates 'to come to be'. The Revised Version translates it 'determination'. In other words, no longer would their inherited skills and expertise be handed down from generation to generation, never again would they pass on abilities that enabled them to establish trades that they alone excelled in. "They shall be *broken* in the *purposes* (*determinations*) thereof, all that make sluices (the skilled) and all that make ponds (the unskilled).

23

Entertainers

Civic Leader

Scientist

It is a well-known fact that many people of different nationalities, the Italians for instance, often pass down lucrative trade secrets to their children from one generation to the next, as do also the Irish people, the Greek, the Japanese, the Chinese and others. However, it is not a general tradition among black people to pass what they know (special abilities and skills) down to the next generation. Consequently Blacks, down through the centuries, have had only a very few accomplishments, by comparison, that they can point to with the kind of racial pride that produces an ethnic and cultural pride as well. Pharaoh couldn't possibly know the long-range consequences this prophecy would bring.

"Surely the princes of Zoan are fools, the counsel of the wise counselors of Pharaoh is become brutish . . ."—Isaiah 19:11a

Zoan was an ancient city of Lower Egypt located in the Delta on the Tanite branch of the Nile. The Lord is said to have worked the wonders of the 10 plagues there (Psalm 78:42–43). Zoan was also the residence of the princes of Egypt. The princes of Zoan were Pharaoh's top counselors, famous for their superior wisdom and foresight. These were the very same counselors the Jews travelled many miles, on foot, to counsel with. Pharaoh never made a single move before he had first consulted with his wise counselors. C. J. Ellicott states: "Egyptian kings, like those in Israel, consulted their prophets before undertaking any expedition." *The counsel of the wise counsellors of Pharoah is become brutish.* The word *brutish* literally means crude, primitive or uncultivated. According to *Vine's,* it comes from the Latin *Brutus,* meaning dull, irrational. God here is threatening to turn the wise counsel of Pharaoh's wise men into foolishness and to make them all look like fools! The prophet warns him that his wise counselors and princes, considered the elite of the wise, would no longer be revered for their superior wisdom but would be ridiculed for their bungling stupidity.

The full understanding of the depth and seriousness of this portion of prophecy necessitates another look back into the history of the Egyptians, because they were a classy, dignified people who had a certain elegance and refinement that was peculiar only to them. Their very appearance exuded confidence and assurance, the enhancement of which gave even more credibility to their counsel. It is a known fact that appearing successful means also looking the part. Their assurance was borne out of knowing that they were the best in the world. After all, did not people come from far and near to counsel with their counselors and wise men? Paul Johnson states it this way: "The essence of Egyptian style can be defined in two words: *majesty* and *self-confidence.* The Egyptians were perhaps the most self-confident people the world has known:

the cultural egocentricity of the later 'Celestial Empire' of China was less exclusive by comparison."

Egypt's Pharaohs throughout history, were credited and praised for the many outstanding achievements and progress of Egypt, yet the real power behind the Pharaohs were their wise men and counselors. Men such as *Imhotep* who himself was not a Pharaoh but was, nevertheless, outstanding in his day as a sage, vizier, astrologer, outstanding architect, physician and chief minister to Pharaoh Djoser. The counselors to the Pharaohs were a lot more than just figure heads. They were selected mainly for their wisdom, knowledge and exceptional abilities. Those who showed true evidence of unusual wisdom, intelligence and spiritual abilities were often used as advisors to the king. Imhotep was such a man. Ancient documents illustrating Egyptian society during the Old Kingdom show that magic and religion were practiced integrally as one method and that the chief magician of the Pharaoh's court also frequently served as the nation's chief physician. The Egyptians' love of any type of display of spiritual wisdom was the reason they never differentiated or distinguished between the spiritual elements of God and the spiritual elements of sorcery. To the Egyptians, both were perfectly acceptable. During the time of Joseph's stay in Egypt, Pharaoh dreamed two dreams which he did not understand, "And it came to pass in the morning that his spirit was troubled; and he sent and called for all the magicians of Egypt, and all the wise men thereof: and Pharaoh told them his dream; but there was none that could interpret them unto Pharaoh." (Genesis 41:1–45). It was Joseph's God-given ability to interpret Pharaoh's dream that not only resulted in his release from prison but he was also appointed superintendent of the royal granaries (Head of the Department of State). Joseph, who was an Israelite, was fully accepted among the Egyptians until the day he died because of his exceptional spiritual abilities.

However, during Isaiah's time, about a thousand years later, the Egyptians' entire way of life was based wholly on sorcery, magicians, and 'wise counselors' whose wisdom depended on witchcraft. ". . . *the counsel of the wise counsellors of Pharaoh is become brutish . . .*"

God warns that the so-called 'wise men and counselors' of Egypt will no longer be classified as wise but will henceforth be made to look very dumb and foolish. No one, ever again, will seek to counsel or confer with them because God shall turn their wisest counsels into foolishness. The confidence placed in the great wisdom and knowledge of Egypt shall be no more. Their leaders can no more be depended upon. Just as Pharaoh had a chief administrator whose job it was to commune between the king and the common people, this method yet exists among the tribes of Africa. The Chief hardly ever speaks directly to the people, but always uses a 'speaker' or communicator who relates to the people what the Chief has to say. It's been said that the Chief really doesn't have to be very intelligent but his communicator is expected to be.

". . . the counsel of the wise counsellors of Pharaoh is become brutish . . ." There is a reiteration of this statement in verse 13 where more shall be discussed on the subject of the counsel of the wise counselors.

". . . how say ye unto Pharaoh. I am the son of the wise, the son of ancient kings?"—Isaiah 19:11b

This particular portion of prophecy is, in my humble opinion, the saddest, most sorrowful and regretful portion of all of the prophecy because God is warning Pharaoh that He shall allow time and circumstances to conceal all knowledge of Egypt's great history and heritage from its descendants. "How say ye unto Pharaoh, *I am the son of the wise, the son of ancient kings?*" Roughly paraphrased, this prophecy would translate like this: "One day you, as a nation and as a people, are going to appear to be so ignorant and backward that it will be hard, next to impossible for anyone to believe that you are the descendants of a great people who were famous for their wisdom and knowledge. (How say ye . . . I am the son of the wise?) You, who started civilization, will appear to be the most uncivilized. Moreover, your descendants will be unable to boast of the fact that they are descended from a long line of great Pharaohs, Kings and Queens. (How say ye . . . I am . . . the son of ancient kings?") Your descendants shall not be able to say with pride, 'I am descended from an ancient royal line honored for their wisdom, abilities and great achievements; I am the descendant of ancient kings.' It is for this reason that the average black person today is not aware of the fact that he is the direct lineal descendant of the great Pharaohs of Egypt! When it comes to any knowledge of cultural heritage, most Blacks can only refer back as far as the Rain Forest.

This prophecy was expected to provoke Pharaoh and kindle his fires of pride because the nobles of Egypt were proud of and boasted much of their antiquity and could produce fabulous records of their successions, going back thousands of years. Their common boast being that Egypt was some thousands of years more ancient than any other nation, believing evidently, that the greatness and power that they were enjoying were going to continue forever. However, God warned Pharaoh, through the prophet Isaiah, that the descending generations to come would not be able to point with pride and confidence to a heritage that no other race on earth can claim. Pharaoh, of course, did not heed the warning, therefore God commenced to allow practically all traces of black people's famous ancestry to be concealed for many, many centuries. It is this fact, exclusively, that accounts for the absence of any mention of black people's great ancestry in the history books and why we have never really understood our place in the scheme of things, thereby never completely knowing ourselves.

The many archaeological discoveries in Egypt that started as far back as the 1700s, make it hard to believe that the English and American historians and archaeologists were not aware of the fact that these same Egyptians, whose tombs they plundered, were the ancestors of the people they held in slavery. Many, not all, of the statues of the Pharaohs that were uncovered possessed the typical dark skin, full lips, broad noses and curly hair. Why was this precious knowledge withheld from black people? *Because God allowed it.* And what about the fact that when the Bible itself was translated into the King James version, the translators did not identify the black people held in slavery with the Egyptians written about in the Bible. Were they aware of the fact? Reverend Walter Arthur McCray, in his book *The Black Presence in the Bible*, seems to think there was an awareness of the fact. He states: "The black presence

A striking view of the Temple of Luxor, with pictured columns and three gigantic statues of the pharaoh Rameses.

was part of the English and colonial scene, but these people were not called "Ethiopians" but "Negroes". Nevertheless, even though the King James translators were aware of the geographical homeland of these black people in the Bible, (the Egyptians) they still called them "Ethiopians". For the term "Ethiopia" did not image a black man to the English reading white mind, but it imaged a "white man in blackish color" due to the hair texture, skin color, Arabian heritage, and geographical location of the modern Ethiopian people . . . Why? Simply because the King James translators refused to identify the black people whom they held as slaves with the black people written about in the Bible. They were motivated by racism, the need to justify slavery and pacify their consciences, and for other socio-economic considerations."

Is it true? Was the knowledge of these things and much more deliberately kept hidden and never mentioned or referred to? Yes! But only because God allowed it in fulfillment of His prophecy. If

30

He had not allowed it, no one could have kept it from being known, no matter what. It is true that while most other nationalities can point to their long line of ancestors that came from England, Ireland, Scotland and Greece, the black man, having no apparent roots, can only relate to the African Rain Forest and slavery, which things do not provide a platform for dignity and respect for one's self. It is this truth, exclusively, that has contributed immensely to the inferiority complex that exists among most black people, although it is widely blamed on the white race. However, it must be understood that God ordained that these things come to pass in order that His prophecy should be fulfilled. Looking back on the prophecy, we can better understand *why* whites were allowed to enslave us, and also to withhold knowledge of our cultural heritage. No nation, not even the mighty Ancient Egyptians, no matter how strong, powerful or wise, can continue to sustain themselves without the true God Jehovah because He is the Master Sustainer. The outright disobedience of our ancestors contributed directly to the fact that our great history has been lost to us for such a long time and that our ancestry was snuffed out and not allowed to follow us throughout the ensuing centuries. "How say ye . . . I am the son of the wise, the son of ancient kings?"

> "Where are they? where are thy wise men? and let them tell thee now, and let them know what the Lord of hosts hath purposed upon Egypt."—Isaiah 19:12

The prophet Isaiah appeals to Pharaoh concerning the so-called wisdom of his soothsayers and wise counselors. 'Where are they? Where are thy wise men?' If they're so wise, why can't they foretell what God "hath purposed upon Egypt?" Let them use their famous abilities to warn of the major changes that are hovering about on the horizon. A time of distress and danger is about to come upon Egypt. Can't they see it? Now is the time to prove their wisdom. Let them show it. Let them declare what is coming

31

upon the nation and begin to take the proper measures necessary to remove it. But if they cannot do this, then Pharaoh should not suffer himself to be deluded, and his kingdom ruined and destroyed forever, by their erroneous counsel.

> "The princes of Zoan are become fools, the princes of Noph are deceived; they have also seduced Egypt, even they that are the stay of the tribes thereof."—Isaiah 19:13

"The princes of Zoan are become fools . . ." The prophet reemphasizes the same statement that he made in verse 11, that all the counselors upon which the Egyptians depended were become fools. Why? Because they had been wholly misled through the sorcerous practices that they had placed all of their faith and trust in. "The princes of Noph are deceived . . ." Egypt shall no longer be distinguished as the very knowledgeable and wise nation it once was, a nation exhibiting a capacity for discernment and the intelligent application of knowledge, but shall seem, to all appearances, to be very foolish and void of understanding.

The motion picture industry played a major part in the fulfillment of this portion of prophecy. In the early years of the industry, movies had a great bearing upon how black people were presented and received in society. Blacks in Africa were, most often, portrayed as ignorant, half-naked natives hauling gear and other supplies for European hunters on safari. Blacks in America were most always cast in subservient, insignificant roles that portrayed them as inferior, lazy, dumb and dishonest or fearful, eye-rolling buffoons. Generally, the roles could be classified either as Toms, Coons, Mulattoes, Mammies, Bucks, pickaninnies, or Uncle Remuses. The characters of the loyal and manageable Toms, the clownish Coons, the fat and hefty Mammies, the troubled and tragic Mulattoes and the brutal black Bucks had all appeared in previous films but had never been given such outstanding, dramatic treatment as in the 1915 movie production of

The Birth of a Nation. The movie gave an in-depth representation of the degraded image of black people at that time in history. These stereotyped impressions, introduced to the mass movie audiences, were to linger long in American films for the next sixty to seventy years, often portraying Blacks as laughable, humorous clowns. "The princes of Zoan are become fools . . ."

Amos 'n Andy

". . . they have also seduced Egypt, even they that are the stay of the tribes thereof." The prophet also points out that it is the erroneous counsel of the *princes* that have caused Egypt to sin and be led into its present state. He is placing the responsibility for Egypt's condition entirely upon the leaders: ". . . *they* have seduced Egypt, *even they that are the stay (leaders, backbone)* of the tribes thereof." *Stay*, in literal terms, means *cornerstones*, that which serves as a support, pillar or foundation. His reference is to the wise men and counselors, sorcerers, magicians, and soothsayers, whose counsel and advice Egypt depended upon. The fact that "they have also seduced Egypt", indicates that the people's minds have already been persuaded and obviously, there's no chance of their ever changing it, preferring to walk in the erroneous counsel and leadership of Egypt's wise men, and be led astray. God's word declares that "Even as they did not like to retain God in their knowledge, God gave them over to a reprobate mind, to do those things which are not convenient." (Romans 1:28). Since Pharaoh and the people chose not to heed the prophet's warning, God gave them over to be led by their 'Wise Men', whose counsels were not based in the word of God. It is a practice that God allowed to become an inherent stronghold among the Egyptian people, a trait that was passed down to their descendants, who, in the past, were so easily swayed under the influence of misguided leaders. The black church, which has been the backbone of the black community for generations, has also , for generations, been the scene of unscrupulous conduct among the leaders, especially the black preachers. Not all of them, thank God, but enough of them, down through the years, that it has practically become customary and traditional in the average black church to find a minister of questionable character presiding over the people as their leader. If he is a drunkard, steals the church's money or is the biggest whoremonger in town, the church will never dismiss him, instead the majority of them will usually follow his lead, and reward his actions with elaborate "anniversaries" every year, not to mention the gifts of fine suits and cars. This type of improper conduct, found commonly in most black churches coast to coast, has been tolerated and allowed to continue in the midst of the black congregation from generation to generation. Question: Why has this practice been tolerated for so long in most black churches? Remember, God gave Egypt over to walk in the counsels of their 'leaders' (princes and counselors), who traditionally honored the elements of good as highly as they honored the elements of evil, never differentiating between the two. Remember, in verse 13, God called the leaders, (princes) *seducers*, which according to *Vine's Expository Dictionary*, is also rendered *imposter*, "which primarily denotes a wailer (goao, to wail); hence from the howl in which spells were chanted, a wizard, sorcerer, enchanter." The A.V. renders it "seducers" or false teachers. Seduce also means, according to *Vine's*, to 'lead astray'. Using the word *seduce*, God clearly reveals that the wise men and magicians of Egypt were able to influence (seduce) the people by using the sway of wailing chants and spells. Much the same way as witch doctors hold sway over the African people by the seductive, wailing monotone of enchantments and spells performed during various ritualistic ceremonies. Similarly, the same power to sway the people (God calls it 'seduce') has traditionally existed among most clergy in many of the black churches of America. If the leader has the ability to speak great swelling words of vanity, accompanied by a 'wailing' type of preaching that appeals to the fleshly senses, he will, most likely, end up leading the people, as they willingly succumb.

"*The princes of Zoan are become fools, the princes of Noph are deceived . . .*" For many centuries after, no man sought the Egyptians for counsel, for their counsel was no longer reliable. This great God-given ability of outstanding wisdom and knowledge was withdrawn by the Great Giver Himself. It is only in recent years that outstanding people of the black race (leaders, if you will) have been elevated into positions where their advice and counsels are accepted and given consideration and credibility.

"*They have also seduced Egypt, even they that are the stay of the tribes thereof.*" Using more modern terms, the scripture would paraphrase like this: "They (the leaders) have also seduced (led astray) Egypt, even they that are the stay (backbone) of the tribes (communities, churches) thereof." This practice started when Pharaoh and the Egyptians chose to follow the counsel of their leaders who were a mixture of princes, wise men, sorcerers and magicians, rather than to heed the counsel of God's prophet, Isaiah. As the prophecy fulfilled over the centuries, God gave them over to their desire and it is an inherent trait that passed down to their descendants. Years ago, in the Old South, it was common to find faithful, church-going black people who also dabbled in a little hoodoo on the side, seeking to persons who could "prophesy" their future in exchange for a few dollars. The common practice was to "run down to Lou'zana to get a quick 'fix' in an effort to put a 'hex' on someone or to find out if a husband, wife, girlfriend or boyfriend was having an affair on the side. There were very few total commitments to faith in God's word because there was always that element of voodoo mixed in with it. This inherent trait, passed down from our ancestors, the Ancient Egyptians, also accounts for the Rock & Roll Kings and the Rhythm & Blues Queens who, for years, have felt quite comfortable performing in the nightclubs as well as in the house of the Lord, singing and recording songs of the world as well as the sacred songs of God sometimes all on the same album! This deadly mixture still exists in some of the Black churches even today.

I'm speaking of these things as if they were in the past because, quite frankly, they are. As I said in the very beginning, all of this prophecy related in this book has been fulfilled and God is now in the process of raising up unto Himself a generation among Blacks who are not looking for a lot of entertainment and insincerity in the church but will be led by His Spirit and not by the corruptions of men.

> "The Lord hath mingled a *perverse spirit* in the midst thereof: and they have caused Egypt to err in every work thereof, as a drunken man staggereth in his own vomit."—Isaiah 19:14

The prophet again warns that God has mixed (mingled) a *perverse spirit* in the midst of the nation. *Perverse* means "to transform into something of an opposite character, to change entirely", signifying a *devolution*. Because of a perverse spirit mingled in the midst of the people, the uniqueness that always distinguished the Egyptians from other nations would one day be just the opposite. The natural nobility and refinement associated with these great people would no longer be an outstanding trait among them. As a matter of fact, it would be the extreme opposite, with unrefinement and undignified behavior becoming a major part of their characteristic makeup. Even the Egyptian culture would no longer

36

be the same. Great knowledge that Egypt once knew, great abilities that they once had would be perverted, lost. ". . . and they have caused Egypt to err in *every work* thereof . . ." Egypt shall never again excel as they once did, as a nation, in any type of work or skill. The word *err*, in literal terms, means to depart from, miss the mark, or deviate from a known standard, miscalculate or fail. These terms, foreign to the nature of the Egyptian, would soon come to be his national trademark. They, who were known for excellence in practically every skill and field known to the ancient world, would no longer be famous for such excellence.

". . . as a drunken man staggereth in his vomit." Another rendering of the word *stagger*, besides the obvious version, is the one that means "An adjustment marked by an *overlapping* arrangement, so that the leading edge of one *projects beyond* the leading edge of another." In a staggered arrangement, objects usually fall *behind* the object just ahead of it, meaning the Egyptians would no longer be in first place but would always fall behind. The word *vomit*, according to *Vine's*, is *to disgorge*. The knowledge and abilities that the Egyptians were outstanding in would be disgorged (vomited), meaning they simply would not stay with them. "As a drunken man staggereth in *his vomit*." In other words, the prophet was declaring that the Egyptians would no longer lead out as before but would stagger (fall behind) in his own vomit (in the very things they had once excelled in.) The Egyptians' mastery in every field of endeavor known to the ancient world, including architecture, sculpture and painting, mathematics, navigation, astronomy, medicine and the industrial arts and sciences, would not be passed down to their descendants. Today, one of Africa's most serious problems is its lack of educated and skilled people. As a whole, it has the lowest literacy rate of any continent. In most African countries only about ten out of every one hundred people can read and write. Until recent times, writing was unknown to most of the people living south of the Sahara.

The many different languages spoken in Africa make the

problem of providing an education for everyone very difficult. Most of the languages have never been written down. In order to go to school, many have to learn another language besides their own. The governments of the African countries are aware of the need for more schools and are having to spend more than 20–3- percent of their national budgets on education. The countries are poor and the budgets small but nevertheless, progress is being made. They, whose ancestors excelled in every major achievement, must now struggle to master them all over again. ". . . They have caused Egypt to err in every work thereof . . ." Because of the lack of education and skills, the native Africans cannot make the electric power, tractors, generators and other equipment needed to develop their own rich mines, forests and other raw materials that Africa possesses in abundance.

In America, where education is available and abundant, the black person yet staggers (falls behind). Even after the slaves were freed, they did not have much chance to move forward. It was not easy for black people to get an education. But now the chances to be educated are far better and the avenues to true freedom in every field are opening and many Blacks are availing themselves of these opportunities. Yet, all across the country, for various reasons, most blacks score the lowest points in academic skills on all levels. Even after over thirty years of integrated education, the majority of black youth are still academically behind. In 1986 the dropout rate for black students was 72 percent for high schools. From the *Sentencing Project*—a nonprofit organization headquartered in Washington D.C., that deals with criminal justice and sentencing reform comes this alarming statistic: ". . . Only 436,000 black males in America in all age groups out of a total of 15 million are attending colleges, universities or other institutions of higher education."

"Neither shall there be *any work* for Egypt, which the head or tail, branch or rush, may do."—Isaiah 19:15

Isaiah prophesies that the day would surely come when it would be very hard and difficult for any Egyptian, head or tail (high or low), branch or rush (great or small) skilled or unskilled, to be able to find work. This portion of prophecy explains the "why" behind the high rate of unemployment among black people. It is usually just as hard for an educated Black to get a job as it is for an uneducated one. The long lines of unemployed black people all across America can surely attest to the fulfillment of this prophecy. In Africa there is serious underemployment, especially of younger people with some education but for whom there is very little skilled work available. Many of the natives work as tenant farmers for European owners, some work the mines, rubber plantations, harbors and the airports, yet 75 percent of all who are able to work, because of low skills, merely scrape out an existence from little plots of land.

This statement from the *Encyclopedia Britannica*: "The most obvious feature of social conditions is the difference between the wages and cost of living of whites and of non-whites. In 1979 the average per capita income for whites was approximately ten times that for Africans . . . The vast majority of Africans have remained untouched by the wage advances in the mining and industrial sectors of the economy. In the early 1980s more than one fourth of the African population was unemployed, and those who were employed were generally in the lowest paying and least prestigious positions."

Back in 1955 black women in America were still doing domestic work for $5.00 a day. Although many new jobs and opportunities have come available in recent years, the unemployment rate among Blacks remains the same. Unemployment among Blacks has almost established itself over the years as an accepted, even expected, conventional tradition. "Neither shall there be any work for Egypt, which the head or tail, branch or rush may do."

"In that day shall Egypt be like unto women: and it shall be afraid and fear because of the shaking of the hand of the Lord of hosts, which He shaketh over it. And the land of Judah shall be a terror

39

unto Egypt, everyone that maketh mention thereof shall be afraid in himself, because of the counsel of the Lord of hosts, which He hath determined against it."—Isaiah 19:16–17

A major element was required to bring about the fulfillment of these prophecies against Pharaoh and the people of Egypt, and that element was *fear*. Fear was needed for two basic reasons: (1) the Egyptians had no fear of their enemies, (2) nor even death itself! The reason they were not fearful of their enemies was because in addition to having bold and courageous soldiers, they also had superior warfare equipment, horses and chariots that were the best made in the world! They knew all about fine horses because the Egyptians were the first to tame the horse for man's use, therefore they were famous for breeding the finest horses that could be had. 2 Chronicles 1:16–17 relates that King Solomon equipped his army with only the best horses and chariots and they all came out of Egypt! "And Solomon *had horses brought out of Egypt*, . . . And they fetched up, and brought forth *out of Egypt* a chariot for 600 shekels of silver, *and an horse* for an hundred and fifty . . ."

The Israelites were often reproved of God for relying on the military might of Egypt. "Woe to them that go down to *Egypt* for help; and stay (place their hope) on *horses*, and trust in *chariots*, because *they are many*; and in *horsemen*, because they are *very strong*; but they look not unto the Holy One of Israel, neither seek the Lord!" (Isaiah 31:1). According to Biblical account, Rabshakeh, captain of the Assyrian armies, once chided Israel for their dependence upon Egypt: "How then wilt thou turn away the face of one captain of the least of my master's servants, and put thy trust on Egypt for chariots and for horsemen?" (2 Kings 18:24). God wanted Israel to put their trust in Him alone and not trust in the might of Egypt's fine chariots and horses. For that reason, one of the duties of a newly elected king of Israel was that ". . . he shall not multiply *horses* to himself, nor cause the people to return to Egypt, *to the end that he should multiply horses* . . ."

(Deuteronomy 17:16). Often the Israelites had to be reminded that Jehovah was their God and not Egypt! "Now the Egyptians are men, and not God; and their horses flesh, and not spirit . . ." (Isaiah 31:3). The Egyptians took great pride in their reputation for fine horses, bred especially for battle. A good war horse, in those days, meant practically everything to a king or a ruler, and a well-made chariot often meant the big difference between victory and defeat. Therefore, with a fine arsenal of 'very strong horsemen', fine horses and chariots, Egypt had no dread fear of their enemies. *"In that day shall Egypt be like unto women: and it shall be afraid and fear because of the shaking of the hand of the Lord of Hosts, which He shaketh over it."*

Also, because the Egyptians were such a dauntless people, it was necessary for God to *implant* fear into their hearts to *make* them afraid, and not only in their hearts, but also into their very nature, because these people were not afraid to die. The Egyptians lived all their lives in preparation for the day of their deaths. Dying, according to their religious beliefs, simply meant moving on to continue life someplace else. The elaborate pyramids and tombs, so famous in Egypt today, were not constructed for the living, but for the dead. Because of their high regard for the dead, the Egyptians furnished their elaborately constructed tombs with all manner of objects used by the dead while they were living. If there were anything that was an obsession with the Egyptians, it was life after death. Most of the pyramids were placed on the west bank of the Nile River, in accordance with their belief that the west, where the sun set, was the land of the dead. They believed that the soul could not exist without the body therefore, every effort had to be made to preserve the corpse through embalming and mummifying. As a final protection, exceedingly splendid tombs were erected to protect the corpse and other burial accompaniments. The only thing the Egyptians had a dread of was dying outside of Egypt, because they thought they would miss eternity.

"In that day shall Egypt . . . be afraid and fear . . . everyone shall be afraid in himself . . ."

Keeping in mind that the Lord had already prophesied that the Egyptians would go into slavery and would be ruled over by cruel and fierce lords, it goes without saying that if a people, such as the Egyptians, were going to be ruled over for such a long period of time, there had to be some fear in their hearts, otherwise they could not be subdued and it would be impossible to continue to rule over them. Many were the times that God would instill fear into the hearts of the enemies of Israel; a fear that was absurd and unreasonable since, in actuality, Israel's enemies far outnumbered them. "This day will I begin *to put the dread of thee and the fear of thee upon the nations that are under the whole heaven; who shall hear report of thee, and shall tremble, and be in anguish of thee."* (Deut. 2:24–25). Many of King David's victories were possible because God placed fear of David into the hearts of the nations. "And the fame of David went out into all lands; and the Lord brought fear of him upon all nations." (1 Chronicles 14:17).

". . . And it shall be afraid and fear because of *the shaking of the hand of the Lord of hosts . . ."* 'The shaking of the hand' is an indication of punishment in the Scriptures and is also usually an indication of anger, or of strong and settled purpose. In other words, in the day that the prophecy shall come to pass, the fear displayed by the Egyptians and their descendants will be there solely for the purpose of bringing to pass that which God has decreed, otherwise it would be, without a doubt, totally impossible for any people or nation to rule over black people. It has been mainly through the power of fear that a minority of Whites in Africa have been able, through the centuries, to rule over a majority of Blacks. Fear has also been the dominating scepter used to rule over black people in America in the past. As the prophecy has been fulfilled, the scepter has also been broken, commencing an era in which fear will no longer dominate the hearts of black people.

A relief from the Temple of Hatshepsut at Deir el-Bahari showing a column of soldiers on the expedition to the Land of Punt, on the horn of Africa.

That God chose the White race, in particular, to fulfill the role of 'cruel lord and fierce king', there can be no doubt, because the fact is that black people are the only race of people that Whites have ever ruled over with any degree of success. There is no record anywhere in known history documenting the fact that any other race, including the Indians, has ever been dominated or ruled over by Whites. And it is this curious fact that helps us to know that white people have not ruled over black people during the past centuries simply because they are White, or superior, or more intelligent than Blacks, but only because God chose to raise up or "stir up" a people who would serve as avengers upon the black person's hard-headed disobedience. The Scriptures relates a similar occurrence where King Solomon also forsook the Lord God and went after other gods, as did Pharaoh and Egypt: "For Solomon went after Ashtoreth, the goddess of the Zidonians, and after Milcom the abomination of the Ammonites. And Solomon did evil in the sight of the Lord, and went not fully after the Lord . . . And the Lord *stirred up* an adversary unto Solomon, Hadad the Edomite . . . And God *stirred him up* another adversary, Rezon the son of Eliadah." No nation of people can expect to escape the judgement of God when they turn away from Him.

> "In that day shall five cities in the land of Egypt speak the language of Canaan, and swear to the Lord of hosts; one shall be called, The City of Destruction. In that day shall there be an altar to the Lord in the midst of the land of Egypt, and a pillar at the border thereof to the Lord.
> And it shall be for a sign and for a witness unto the Lord of hosts in the land of Egypt: *For they shall cry unto the Lord because of the oppressors, and he shall send them a saviour, and a great one, and he shall deliver them.*—Isaiah 19:18–20

The prophet foretells that in the day of fulfillment there would be a recognition of Jehovah God and an embracing of the true religion in the land of Egypt, the land where there was once no recognition of God at all. The beginning of the fulfillment of this prophecy is apparent from history. During the time that Alexander the Great took possession of Egypt, about 332 B.C., large numbers of Jews were transplanted and settled in Egypt. Under Alexander and the Ptolemies, who later succeeded him, the Jews were favored, especially by the Ptolemies, and were granted many privileges. The Jews became so numerous that it became necessary that their Scriptures be translated into Greek and the translation called the Septuagint was made. The number of the Jews in Egypt were not less than one million and they were settled in nearly all parts of Egypt, especially in Migdol, Tahpanes, Noph called Memphis and Thebes, known biblically as No or No-Amon, and particularly in Heliopolis (the five cities referred to in verse 18). Heliopolis is the Greek name for the city of Onu, meaning "pillar city" because it was the seat of the worship of the sun god Amon-Re, and it was the most corrupt.

'The language of Canaan' evidently refers to the Hebrew language which is used to denote that they would be converted to the Jewish religion, "swear to the Lord of hosts", and devote themselves to Him and His service. The word 'altar' indicates there would be a general place of worship established, and a pillar' refers to a stone or column of wood erected as a monument or memorial or some type of manifestation of God, such as the sign of the cross, and it shall be for a sign and for a witness unto the Lord of hosts in the land of Egypt. The cross would be a sign of divine hope symbolizing the death, burial and resurrection of Jesus Christ, and when "they shall cry unto the Lord because of the oppressors", they who shall look to the sign of the cross of Jesus Christ would be delivered from the bonds of oppression. It's interesting that the two countries of Africa that are considered Christian countries, Ethiopia and Liberia, have never been under foreign rule. In 1821 many old, ill and unwanted slaves were sent back to Africa after slavery was abolished and profits from the business began to fall off sharply. In 1822 a group of Christian Negroes, freed slaves from America, embarked for western Africa and founded the country of Liberia. Christianity probably reached Ethiopia in the fourth century and, to this day, has remained basically Christian. In the last half of the nineteenth century a number of European countries took over enormous sections of the African continent. When the rush was over only ancient Ethiopia and the Negro Republic of Liberia amazingly, were still wholly independent. The rest of the great continent had been parceled out among France, Britain, Portugal, Italy, Germany, Belgium, Spain and the Union of South Africa.

". . . and He shall send them a saviour . . ." In other words, it shall be through the death, burial and resurrection of Jesus Christ that the power of the prophecy shall be wholly broken because he shall be the only deliverer from the continued consequences of the prophecy. The full understanding of this passage is discussed in the summary.

It is so clear why God has, for centuries, designated so many Christian missionaries to carry the Gospel of Jesus Christ to Africa, that the worship of the true God would be established in the land, just as He promised. And He is yet continuing to do so. The freedom that black people of America have today is due to the fact that the Civil Rights Movement was based entirely out of the Black churches, through the earnest and sincere prayers of thousands of Egyptian descendants, Negroes, as they were called, who had placed their faith in the one God and His Son, Jesus Christ. Pastors and ministers of the traditional Baptist faith, who had the courage to believe that the one God they had trusted all the many years, really wanted them to be free, stepped out and brought to pass through non-violence, the thing that God had already decreed was theirs through His Son, Jesus Christ.

"And the Lord shall be known to Egypt, and the Egyptians shall know the Lord in that day, and shall do sacrifice and oblation; yea, they shall vow a vow unto the Lord, and perform it."—Isaiah 19:21

Isaiah prophesies that not only would the Egyptians be converted to know the true God but would also offer sacrifices and oblations unto Jehovah. The sense is that they would be true worshippers of God through the knowledge of the Jewish faith, which was introduced into the land of Egypt even before the coming of

Christ! "Yea, they shall vow a vow unto the Lord, and perform it.", most likely meaning they traveled to Jerusalem as often as was necessary to observe with the Jews the customary rites of their religion, including the celebration of Pentecost.

As far back as the first century A.D., history records that the Jews were actively engaged in making converts to the Jewish faith. Jesus Himself commended the Scribes and Pharisees for the fact that they "compass sea and land to make one proselyte (convert). (Matthew 23:15). The results of their active campaigning for converts explain why that in the second chapter of Acts, on the day of Pentecost. ". . . devout men, *out of every nation under heaven . . .*" were there, including the land of *Egypt!* ". . . Phrygia, and Pamphylia, *in Egypt, and in the parts of Libya about Cyrene . . .*" (Acts 2:10). And among them also was a certain man of Ethiopia, an eunuch of great authority under Candace, Queen of the Ethiopians, who had charge of all her treasure. This Ethiopian, no doubt, had already been converted by the Jews in his homeland of Ethiopia, Africa and "had come to Jerusalem for to worship", as probably was his custom. On his way back to Ethiopia. he met Phillip who explained the way of the cross to him and led him to believe in Jesus Christ as his Saviour, ". . . and he went on his way rejoicing." As a result, Ethiopia became the first Black Christian country on the continent of Africa because, according to tradition, this very man returned to Ethiopia and was instrumental in converting the Queen of Ethiopia! Today Christians are generally believed to constitute about half the population in Ethiopia. An estimated 35 percent are Muslims and the remainder are mostly animists. The Ethiopian Orthodox Christian Church is the established church and has been viewed in Ethiopian history as the prime source and custodian of the cultural and literary heritage of the country.

It's interesting to note that these happenings occurred before the Muslims came to Africa and before the White slave traders began to enslave African men and women. And although the majority of the population of Africa remained pagan, the main exception was the strong Coptic Christian Church of Ethiopia. The claim that Christianity was introduced to Black people by a few compassionate White slave masters is just not true. God had begun fulfilling His prophecy long before Blacks came to America as slaves.

> "And the Lord shall smite Egypt: he shall smite and heal it: and they shall return even to the Lord, *and He shall be intreated of them, and shall heal them.*"—Isaiah 19:22

In this portion of prophecy given to Isaiah, God predestines that one day true and total deliverance would come to Egyptian descendants. The prophecy against the Black man cannot continue indefinitely because God never intended that it should last forever, "And the Lord shall smite Egypt: *He shall smite and heal it.*" For many generations the state of the black race has been considered as an eternal curse that God placed upon them because their ancestor, Ham, looked upon the nakedness of his father, Noah. However, it is generally accepted that a curse is an evil placed upon mankind from which there is no deliverance as long as this world stands. For instance, the curse that God placed upon mankind after Adam and Eve sinned in the garden is a curse that is yet in effect and shall remain so until Jesus Christ comes back again. The state of the Black race, however, is not the result of a curse, but it was *a prophecy against the black race*, and a prophecy, once it is fulfilled, includes an end. It is the same as when God prophesied to Abraham that Israel, his descendants, would one day go into slavery, ". . . and they shall be afflicted 400 years . . . and *afterward* shall they come out with great substance." (Gen. 15:13–14). God has dealt with the Egyptians for their sin of turning away from Him; now He is in the process of healing (restoring) them. He has always had a day of deliverance set for black people to be free again. ". . . and they shall return even to the Lord. and He shall be intreated of them, *and shall heal them.*" Black

48

people who seek total freedom (spiritually as well as culturally) will obtain it only through God's Son, Jesus Christ. If African Blacks should ever obtain the total freedom they seek for the continent, even after apartheid has been abolished, it will be after they, too, have come together in the power of the one God Jehovah, and His Son Jesus Christ.

> "In that day shall there be a highway out of Egypt to Assyria, and the Assyrian shall come into Egypt, and the Egyptians shall serve with the Assyrians. In that day shall Israel be the third with Egypt ·and with Assyria, even a blessing in the midst of the land: Whom the Lord of hosts shall bless, saying, Blessed be Egypt my people, and Assyria the work of my hands and Israel mine inheritance."—
> Isaiah 19:23–25

There shall be a common goal. Egypt, alongside other nations, shall worship the same God, serving Him united as one people (Christians) in the service of the true God. A unity not based on any political or civil alliance but in the same army of God, under the same leader, Jesus Christ.

Summary

Like Daniel, who through the interpretation of Nebuchadnezzar's dream, was able to see events far into the future, even into the latter days—so was the prophet Isaiah allowed to gaze into the future of the Egyptian people, spanning the time from the beginning of the prophecy, through the centuries, to its fulfillment, even to this very day. In summarizing this portion of the prophecy given to Isaiah in a sort of nutshell form, it is clear that the warning was intended to *describe* the calamities that would come upon Egypt, and the long-range effects they would have upon the people as a nation and the land, if they did not repent and turn back to God. However, because Pharaoh and the Egyptians failed to heed the prophet's warning, God allowed the fullness of the prophecy to fall on the Egyptians and their descendants (African black people).

1. "Behold, the Lord rideth upon a swift cloud, and shall come into Egypt: and the idols of Egypt shall be moved at His presence . . ." The prophet sees God's destruction coming swiftly in a cloud (history records it as an earthquake) destroying the idols of that nation. The Egyptians took the greatest pains to make the temples of their gods beautiful. The largest and one of the most splendid, the Temple of Ammon at Thebes, took almost four hundred years to build. Although it is now in ruins, it yet remains one of the chief wonders of Ancient Egyptian architecture.

2. "And I will set the Egyptians against the Egyptians: and they shall fight every one against his brother . . . against his neighbor . . . city against city, and kingdom against kingdom." A spirit of disunity and discord would exist among the Egyptians and their descendants. 'Egyptians against the Egyptians'. There would be an inability to come together and cooperate together as one people. The situation surrounding the conflicts between Blacks and Oriental immigrants who migrate to the U.S. is a point worth considering. Each new group of foreigners (Vietnamese, Korean, etc.) arrives with nothing, scratching for a foothold. The whole family comes together willing to toil for incredibly long hours for low wages in order to finally begin to succeed after what sometimes seems an unbelievably short period of time. However, their success stirs the resentment of the long-time Black residents in the neighborhood whose ill-will stems from the immigrants' ability to garner profits from their community. The Blacks, some of whom are members of the working class or are desperately poor, figure they should be running what seems to be a highly lucrative enterprise. But when asked why they, who are the long-time residents, have never come together and attempted such an endeavor, they, most often can give no clear-cut answer. ". . . And I will set the Egyptians against the Egyptians."

3. ". . . And they shall seek to the idols, and to the charmers and to them that have familiar spirits, and to the wizards." As a consequence of their disobedience, the Egyptians were given over to the practice of sorcery, from which came voodoo, hoodoo, Black magic, and other beliefs that still persists among many Blacks all over the world. The use of voodoo dolls and images that are believed to place a "hex" or "cast a spell" on an enemy, was derived from an Egyptian ritual that the Egyptian people used against their enemies. According to ancient Egyptian texts called *Execration Texts*, this ritual was done with human figures made of clay or red pottery bowls. Each object was inscribed with the name of the enemy of the Pharaoh and also inscribed with cursings against the enemy. The object was then ceremonially thrown down and crushed, signifying the crushing of all opposition against the king.

The snake is a major object used in the practice of sorcery. The Egyptian Pharaoh's headdress or crown differed from that of all other countries because the snake or sacred cobra, called the Uraeus, was erected in the middle of the forehead. The belief was that it would spit at anyone who came too near to the Pharaoh. ". . . and they shall seek to the idols . . . charmers . . . familiar spirits . . . wizards."

4. "and the Egyptians will I give over into the hand of a cruel Lord; and a fierce King shall rule over them . . ." God warned that He would allow the Egyptians to go into slavery and be ruled over by merciless and cruel people. The annals and chronicles of the past have borne out the fulfillment of this prophecy. It is the only portion of black people's past that can be found in the history books.

5. "and the waters shall fail from the sea, and the river shall be wasted and dried up . . ." It is the fulfillment of this portion of the prophecy that accounts for the extreme drought condition

51

that exists in Africa today. It also accounts for the many deserts that are present on the continent and why they are continuing to expand.

6. **"Moreover they that work in fine flax, and they that weave networks, shall be confounded, and they shall be broken in the purposes thereof . . ."** The ability to excel in the finer skills (the sciences, architecture, fine linen weaving, goldsmithing, jewelry-making, etc.) would no longer be the trademark of Egyptians nor their descendants.

7. **"Surely the princes of Zoan are fools, the counsel of the wise counselors of Pharaoh is become brutish."** The Egyptians and their descendants would no longer be widely known and honored for their exceptional mastery of wisdom and knowledge, but would appear foolish with a lack of refinement.

8. **". . . How say ye unto Pharaoh, I am the son of the wise, the son of ancient Kings?"** The black person's knowledge of his or her ancestry would be concealed and not made known to him for many centuries, which accounts for the fact that black people are not aware of their true origin.

9. **"The Lord hath mingled a perverse spirit in the midst . . . they have caused Egypt to err in every work thereof, as a drunken man staggereth in his vomit."** A perverse spirit meaning a contrary nature that would be just the opposite of the typical Egyptian nature. The Egyptians' character, behavior and total way of life would be counter in every way. A people of class and elegance would now be a people of a low, crude, unrefined nature.

10. **"Neither shall there be any work for Egypt, which the head or tail, branch or rush may do."** God warned that the day would come when Egypt would look for work but wouldn't be able to

find any. The incredible unemployment rate among Blacks across America and in Africa gives unquestioned credibility of the fulfillment of this prophecy.

11. "In that day shall Egypt . . . be afraid and fear . . ." Faintheartedness, timidity and fearfulness would become a characteristic of the nature of the Egyptian and his descendant.

12. ". . . for they shall cry unto the Lord because of the oppressors, and he shall send them a Saviour and a great one, and he shall deliver them." Isaiah prophesies that although God will punish Egypt's sin, He shall also heal His people and return them back to Himself. They shall cry out to Him because of their oppressors (those who deal harassment, injustice, persecution, cruelty) and He shall send them a Saviour and a Great One and He shall deliver them. An explanation of "a Saviour" and a "Great One" is in order at this point in the exposition because the Hebrew translation of both "Saviour" and "Great One" renders them, not as one and the same person but as two *different* people, functioning in two *different roles*, even at two *different times!* Several Bible commentaries and many theologians basically agree that a "Saviour" is in reference to the Messiah, Jesus Christ, whose function is basically, a spiritual deliverance; and that He, essentially, must appear upon the scene *before the* "Great One". Since God is speaking of a *total* freedom of the black race, spiritual freedom would certainly be a prerequisite. However, who the "Great One" would be, has been a subject on which there has been a great deal of controversy.

Many opinions have been submitted, however, the most popular belief is that the "Great One" is in reference to Alexander the Great who took possession of Egypt and was regarded by the Egyptians as a sort of deliverer. According to history, the Egyptians, out of hatred of the Persians, submitted cheerfully to Alexander, so that he became master of the country without any

Martin Luther King Jr. 1929–1968

opposition. It is reported that he treated them with much kindness and during his reign, commerce again flourished, trade revived and peace and plenty was in the land. However, when Alexander came on the scene, the prophecy was yet in its beginning stages and even during and after his short reign in Egypt, the once famous culture of the Egyptians had begun to deteriorate, finally ending in slavery which began as early as the 1400s, continuing over a period of over 400 years. Therefore, Alexander the Great could not have been the *great one* designated to deliver the Egyptians. In the Hebrew interpretation, it is evident that a person is here denoted who would be sent *after* the national judgements God had prophesied upon Egypt. It is in the sense that a deliverer would appear on the scene *after* the complete fulfillment of the prophecy and would be instrumental in their final delivery.

In other words, the entry of the *great one* would signal the end or completion of the prophecy and the beginning of absolute freedom for black people. Therefore, the *great one* spoken of would certainly have to be in reference to Dr. Martin Luther King, Jr., because although black people had freedom in the form of an official document (the Constitution of the United States), yet they experienced no real freedom until, through the providence of God, Dr. King was raised up. His entrance upon the scene signified the fulfillment of the prophecy and its ending.

In Genesis 15:13–16 God warned Abraham that the Israelites would surely one day go into bondage but He also set the time that they would be delivered. "And He said unto Abram, Know of a surety that thy seed shall be a stranger in a land that is not theirs, and shall serve them; and they shall afflict them *four hundred years . . . but in the fourth generation they shall come hither again . . .*" And Moses was not raised up as a deliverer until *after* the four hundred years of slavery were fulfilled. It is no coincidence that Dr. King was a minister of the Gospel for he was the true one that God chose to deliver black people, otherwise the movement would have failed and been listed among the many other uprisings that preceded it in history past. It was not simply another attempt to be free but because God had already ordained the day of freedom, Dr. King's efforts not only remained, but also afforded a freedom that black Americans had not experienced since they left the Bush and Rain Forests of Africa! It is a freedom that has slowly but continually progressed as more and more Blacks are free to achieve in fields that once were closed to them. It must be noted that by the time Dr. King arrived on the scene, God had already raised up a generation whose minds were no longer bound and whose hearts were set for freedom. Beginning with the Alabama Bus Boycott in 1955, the old spirit of disunity had already begun to slowly diminish among black people. Sadly, many Blacks will remain "down on the plantation", and will refuse, for fear, to walk in the freedom provided. But the ones who are succeeding are the ones who have chosen to cast off the old "slave mentality" that yet clings to many black people.

Although black people, as a nation, will never again rule over other nations as a world power, as did their ancestors, the Ancient Egyptians, they will again excel and be great, not as a nation, but as a people and as a race.

Isaiah Chapter 20

It is recorded that this portion of prophecy was given to Isaiah in the very same year as the first one, 713 B.C., perhaps a few months later. In this part of the prophecy God places strong emphasis upon the fact that the land of Egypt and all its inhabitants are destined for slavery. However, the most remarkable peculiarity that makes this part of the prophecy extraordinary is the resolute obedience of the prophet Isaiah as he is commanded to walk naked and barefoot before the Egyptians for three years as a sign to them of their pending destiny. Less drastic measures surely may have sufficed but the fact that God commands the prophet to do this for three long years is indicative of God's great reluctance to follow through with what He has determined shall be.

There had always been long intimate contact between the dark skinned Egyptians and the dark-skinned Ethiopians. They traded and intermarried for more than fifty centuries and were often united in an alliance. Both Egypt and Ethiopia are named in the prophecy, indicating that God is referring to the entire land of Egypt!

> "In the year that Tartan came unto Ashdod (when Sargon the king of Assyria sent him), and fought against Ashdod and took it; At the same time spake the Lord by Isaiah the son of Amoz, saying, Go and loose the sackcloth from off thy loins, and put off thy shoe from thy foot. And he did so, walking naked and barefoot. And the Lord said, Like as my servant Isaiah hath walked naked and barefoot three years *for a sign and wonder upon Egypt and Ethiopia*; So shall the king of Assyria lead away the Egyptians prisoners, and the Ethiopians captives, young and old, naked and barefoot, *even with their buttocks uncovered*, to the shame of Egypt."—Isaiah 20:1–4

Isaiah is to be applauded and commended for obedience and faithfulness beyond the call of duty. His walking naked and barefoot before the Egyptians was designed to emphasize the fact that they, "young and old", would one day be stripped of all their possessions and carried, "naked and barefoot", as captives and prisoners into slavery.

Isaiah had orders from God to "loosen his sackcloth from his loins". This action was not only to be a sign to them but it was a wonder as well because of the fact that Isaiah was no common, ordinary dirt farmer suddenly called by God to go and prophesy! When he was first called to the office of prophet, he was already a High Priest serving in the temple of God. Jewish writers constantly affirm that he was of noble extraction and closely connected with the royal family. The fact that he was admitted so freely into the counselings of kings may seem to give some credence to this idea. He discharged his prophetic office under the reigns of kings Uzziah, Jothem, Ahaz, and Hezekiah. Evidently, he was an educated man because many writers have highly esteemed his style, declaring that, ". . . in his discourse he is so eloquent, and is a man of so noble and refined elocution, without any mixture of rusticity that it is impossible to preserve or transfuse the beauty of his style in a translation." Isaiah has been considered the most sublime of all the Bible writers. His styles, thoughts, images and expressions have been regarded as poetical, and that in the highest degree.

The eloquence and nobility of the man Isaiah was quite obvious and for that reason, he was the perfect choice for God's purpose because the Egyptian people, themselves, were an eloquent and noble people. Therefore, the symbolic action of Isaiah, the eloquent, the noble, walking naked and barefoot in public for three years was a profound and serious warning to the Egyptians that, "Like as my servant Isaiah, hath walked naked and barefoot for a sign and a wonder upon Egypt and upon Ethiopia, so shall the king of Assyria lead away the Egyptians prisoners, and the Ethiopians captives, young and old, naked and barefoot, even with their buttocks uncovered, to the shame of Egypt."

In the end this prophecy was wholly fulfilled with the advent of slave traders who kidnapped and captured millions of Africans. As early as the 11th century A.D. there lived a slave raider named Sultan Samory who lived along the upper Niger River and had captured and sold about a million and a half black slaves to the Tuaregs, a nomadic people, in exchange for gold, cattle and ivory. The big-eared elephants that abounded in the region were frequently slaughtered for their tusks of white ivory, and long processions of slaves, who themselves were headed to market to be sold, were forced to carry these tusks upon their shoulders, *walking naked and barefoot*. The black slaves were called "Black Ivory".

Isaiah's walking naked and barefoot for three years was, indeed, a strong warning to Egypt but the seriousness of the prophet's message went unheeded, and consequently, the prophecy fell on the Egyptians and their descendants. To this day, tribes in the bush of Africa wear scarcely any clothes. Many, when discovered, have customarily been naked and barefoot all their lives, with no concept of what it means to wear clothes. The little that is worn is generally made of whatever materials are at hand, often grasses or animal skins.

The African slave trade thrived for over 400 years and often the slaves were forced to be auctioned on the auction block, bunched together like animals, "naked and barefoot, with their buttocks uncovered. to the shame of Egypt."

> "And they shall be afraid and ashamed of Ethiopia their expectation and Egypt their glory. And the inhabitant of this isle shall say in that day, Behold, such is our expectation, whither we flee for help to be delivered from the king of Assyria: and how shall we escape?"—Isaiah 20:5–6

So great were the powers and influence of this nation of black people that they were the object of glory for other nations that boasted of their alliance with Egypt and Ethiopia, believing that neither the people nor the country could ever be overthrown and brought to its knees. But they would begin to fear and be amazed that a great and mighty people as the Egyptians could be vanquished and brought down to such a state! "Ethiopia their expectation, Egypt their glory!"

Chapter 2

Jeremiah Chapters 43, 44 & 46

After the Lord sent Isaiah to the reigning Pharaoh, who is believed to have been Sheshonq II, He now, 125 years later (607 B.C.), speaks to the prophet, Jeremiah. God warns the Jews, who are determined to enter into Egypt and dwell there "to burn incense and to serve other gods", that Egypt is no longer a haven of safety for them. God warns He is preparing to destroy the Egyptians and their gods. He plans to send Nebuchadnezzar, king of Babylon, whom He will use as an instrument to commence to execute His will against the Egyptians. ". . . Behold, I will send and take Nebuchadnezzar the king of Babylon . . . and when he cometh, he shall smite the land of Egypt . . ." (Jeremiah 43:10–11).

The prophet Jeremiah also warns, as did Isaiah, that Egypt shall one day go into slavery, "O, thou daughter dwelling in Egypt, *furnish thyself to go into captivity* . . ." (Jeremiah 46:19). He prophesies of famine and drought, ". . . for Noph shall be waste and desolate without an inhabitant." (Jeremiah 46:19b). Even the invasion of the Europeans, who once controlled most of the continent of Africa, was prophesied: ". . . but destruction cometh; it cometh *out of the North.*" (Jeremiah 46:20). "The daughter of Egypt shall be confounded; she shall *be delivered into the hand of the people of the North.*" (Jeremiah 46:24).

This portion of prophecy given to Jeremiah marks the beginning of the end of the supreme power Egypt has enjoyed for thousands of years. One after another the nations have been consumed by Nebuchadnezzar, and now his forces are about to fall upon Egypt. In spite of all their elaborate preparations for this particular battle, Jeremiah warns that they shall be shamefully defeated, for, having now fallen out of the divine favor of God, He would now fight against them:

The multitude of the city of Noph, called populous No in Nahum 3:8, shall be desolate, without an inhabitant. The name Pharaoh, synonymous with power and glory, is now just an enpty noise, nothing now remains but his ruin. "They did cry there, Pharaoh, king of Egypt is but a noise; he hath passed the time appointed." (Jeremiah 46:17).

The Great Battle at Carchemish

125 years later (607 B.C.) the Lord speaks to the prophet Jeremiah concerning Egypt. At this time the Israelites, in an effort to escape undesirable conditions that existed in Judah, have determined to enter into Egypt to dwell there "to burn incense and to serve other gods". Jeremiah has received word from God that it is not a wise decision, that Egypt is no longer a haven of safety for them because God is about to destroy the Egyptians and their gods. "If ye wholly set your faces to enter into Egypt, and go to sojourn there; Then it shall come to pass, that the sword, which ye feared, shall overtake you there in the land of Egypt, and the famine, whereof ye were afraid, shall follow close after you there in Egypt; and there ye shall die . . ." (Jeremiah 42:15b–16). The Jews have only contempt for the message and denies it to be the word of God.

"So they came into the land of Egypt: for they obeyed not the voice of the Lord: thus came they even to Tahpanhes. Then came the word of the Lord unto Jeremiah in Tahpanhes, saying, Take great stones in thine hand, and hide them in the clay in the brick kiln, which is at the entry of Pharaoh's house in Tahpanhes, in the sight of the men of Judah; And say unto them, Thus saith the Lord of hosts, the God of Israel; Behold I will send and take Nebuchadnezzar the king of Babylon, my servant, and will set his throne upon these stones that I have hid; and he shall spread his royal pavilion over them. And when he cometh, *he shall smite the land of Egypt*, and deliver such as are for death to death; and such as are for captivity to captivity; and such as are for the sword to the sword."—Jeremiah 43:7–11

Although Jeremiah reluctantly enters into Egypt with the Israelites, God again comes to him with a warning which is also a prophecy concerning the destruction of Egypt. He was commanded to take great stones and lay them beside the way that leads to Pharaoh's house, *in the sight of the men of Judah*, so that when Nebuchadnezzar conquers Egypt and sets his throne in that very place where the stones were laid, the people might be confirmed in their belief of God's word.

> "And I will kindle a fire in the houses of the gods of Egypt; and he shall burn them, and carry them away captives: and he shall array himself with the land of Egypt, as a shepherd putteth on his garment; and he shall go forth from thence in peace. He shall break also the images of Bethshemesh, that is in the land of Egypt; and the houses of the gods of the Egyptians shall he burn with fire."—Jeremiah 43:12–13

Once again God reinforces His determination to destroy the idols, temples (houses) and gods of the Egyptians and Nebuchadnezzar shall be used as His instrument. ". . . and he shall array himself with the land of Egypt . . ." This outstanding conquest of Egypt by Nebuchadnezzar would stand out amidst all his other conquests, placing quite a feather in his cap. The pride and glory that accompanies the triumph of a great victory over the mighty Egyptians shall be his, with all the bluster and exaltation that goes with it. So easily shall the king of Babylon take possession of all the glory of Egypt, ". . . as a shepherd putteth on his garment . . .", and shall depart with out any resistance, ". . . and he shall go forth from thence in peace."

"Thus saith the Lord; Behold, I will give *Pharaoh Hophra* king of Egypt into the hand of his enemies, and into the hand of them that seek his life; as I gave Zedekiah king of Judah into the hand of Nebuchadnezzar king of Babylon, his enemy, and that sought his life."—Jeremiah 44:30

"The word of the Lord which came to Jeremiah the prophet against the Gentiles; Against Egypt, against the army of Pharaoh-*Necho* king of Egypt, which was by the *River Euphrates in Carchemish*, which Nebuchadnezzar king of Babylon smote in the fourth year of Jehoiakim the son of Josiah king of Judah."—Jeremiah 46:1–2

It is notable that the word of the Lord came to Jeremiah with a message for Pharaoh-Hophra during his reign, and later to Pharaoh-Necho also during his reign. The dates are uncertain, but possibly a grace period of perhaps twenty years or more intervened between these predictions. However, it is fairly certain that between the years 605–586 B.C., Nebuchadnezzar defeated Pharaoh-Necho at Carchemish. History records it this way: "During the reign of (Pharaoh) Necho, Egypt supported Assyria as a buffer against the potential threat of the Medes and the Babylonians. Necho was successful in Palestine and Syria until 605 B.C., when the Babylonian Nebuchadnezzar inflicted a severe defeat on Egyptian forces at Carchemish." (*1983 Encyclopaedia Britannica*).

The interesting fact is that Jeremiah's prophecy was given about two years before the battle at Carchemish. One after another the nations had been defeated by Nebuchadnezzar. Tyre, which so long had withstood him, had fallen, and now his forces were about to fall upon Egypt. The prophet warned that all of their preparations for this battle would be of no avail for God Himself was against the Egyptians:

"Order ye the buckler and shield, and draw near to battle. Harness the horses; and get up, ye horsemen, and stand forth with your

64

helmets; furbish the spears, and put on the brigadines. Wherefore have I seen them dismayed and turned away back? and their mighty ones are beaten down, and are fled apace, and look not back: for fear was round about, saith the Lord. Let not the swift flee away, nor the mighty man escape; they shall stumble, and fall toward the north by the river Euphrates. Who is this that cometh up as a flood, whose waters are moved as the rivers? Egypt riseth up like a flood, and his waters are moved like the rivers; and he saith, I will go up, and will cover the earth; I will destroy the city and the inhabitants thereof."—Jeremiah 46:3–8

He compares this expedition to the rising of the river Nile, "Egypt riseth up like a flood . . ." threatening to overflow all the neighboring lands: ". . . I will go up and cover the earth . . ." The advance of the Egyptian army as they march out of Egypt arranged in three divisions, cavalry, chariots and infantry, is described as they begin their campaign:

"Come up, ye horses: and rage ye chariots; and let the mighty men come forth; the Ethiopians and Libyans, that handle the shield; and the Lidians, that handle and bend the bow."—Jeremiah 46:9

As they march forth in haughty confidence, their famous horses and chariots cannot deliver them in this battle for they shall be shamefully defeated. All victories in battles that had been won prior to this battle were because of God's favor towards the Egyptians. He had chosen to exalt them above all the other nations, giving them divine favor even in their encounters against their enemies. However, this shall be no more, attesting to the soverign power of Almighty God who is in control of everything.

Since the Egyptians were widely acclaimed for their famous horses trained specially for battle, it's interesting just how well trained these horses really were. A well-trained war horse was taught many techniques that often resulted in actually saving the life of its rider. For instance, the horse was trained to kick out with his front legs to ward off the foot soldiers around him and come back down on his front legs and kick out his hind legs to also ward off the enemy. An incredible feat and all without losing his rider! The world famous *Lipizzaner Stallions* give a fine illustration of this remarkable accomplishment. The horse had to be sensitive to the least touch of the knee or the foot since its rider sometimes had to free up his hands to handle the sword or spear. They were also taught special steps and prancings designed to enhance the rider, especially the King, as he rode in victory parades after a great triumph. Chariots were not only very efficient but they were also very appealing to the eye. In the burial chambers of King Tutankhamen, two of the rooms were crowded with, among other things, chariots. These chariots are very beautiful and heavily encrusted with gold.

". . . Let the mighty men come forth; the Ethiopians and the Libyans . . . and the Lydians . . ." Their neighbor and ally, the Ethiopians, and their auxilliary forces, the Libyans and the Lydians, their neighbor to the west of Egypt, represented a very formidable army but in vain:

> "For this is the day of the Lord God of hosts, a day of vengeance, that he may avenge him of his adversaries: and the sword shall devour, and it shall be satiate and made drunk with their blood: for the Lord God of hosts hath a sacrifice in the north country by the river *Euphrates*. Go up into Gilead, and take balm, O virgin, the daughter of Egypt: in vain shalt thou use many medicines; *for thou shalt not be cured.* The nations have heard of thy shame, and thy cry hath filled the land: for the mighty man hath stumbled against the mighty, and they have fallen both together."
> —Jeremiah 46:10

The loss sustained by this defeat disabled the Egyptians and, except for a few small skirmishes, were never again able to make any attempts upon other nations again. ". . . in vain shalt thou use many medicines; *for thou shalt not be cured.*" Sorely wounded, they were never able to bring such a powerful army into the field again. *The nations have heard of thy shame, and thy cry hath filled the land . . .*" The nations that once exulted of the glory, strenghth and power of Egypt have now heard of thy disgrace, how shamefully thou wast beaten and how thou art weakened by it.

> "The word that the Lord spake to Jeremiah the prophet, how Nebuchadnezzar king of Babylon should come and smite the land of Egypt. Declare ye in Egypt, and publish in Migdol, and publish in Noph and in Tahpanhes: say ye, stand fast, and prepare thee; for the sword shall devour round about thee. Why are thy valiant men swept away? *They stood not, because the Lord did drive them. He made many to fall, yea, one fell upon another*: and they said, Arise, and let us go again to our own people, and to the land of our nativity, from the oppressing sword. They did cry there, Pharaoh king of Egypt is but a noise; he hath passed the time appointed. As I liveth, saith the King, whose name is the Lord of hosts, Surely as Tabor is among the mountains, and as Carmel by the sea, so shall he come"—Jeremiah 46:13–18

Jeremiah is commanded to 'declare in Egypt . . . Migdol . . . Noph . . . and Tahpanhes' that the sword is coming but Egypt shall be soundly beaten for God Himself shall fight against them: ". . . they stood not, because the Lord did drive them. He made many to fall, yea, one fell upon another . . ."

"They did cry there, Pharaoh king of Egypt is but a noise . . ." The great name of Pharaoh that formerly struck fear in the hearts of enemies, the name synonymous with power and glory, is now just an empty noise, nothing remains but his ruin. Apries, a later Pharaoh, was deposed about 569 B.C. by Ahmose II. However, in 525 B.C. his son and successor Psamtik III was conquered by Cambyses II, king of Persia. With this final defeat came the beginning of the collapse of Egyptian government, culture and independence. Egypt became a province of Persia,and was ruled for nearly two centuries by Persian kings. No native Egyptian king ever ruled in Egypt again. ". . . he hath passed the time appointed." Gone forever are the days of Egyptian greatness, excellence and power.

"O thou daughter dwelling in Egypt, furnish thyself *to go into captivity*: for Noph shall be waste and desolate without an inhabitant. Egypt is like a very fair heifer, but destruction cometh; *it cometh out of the North.* Also her hired men are in the midst of her like fatted bullocks; for they also are turned back, and are fled away together: they did not stand, because the day of their calamity was come upon them, and the time of their visitation."—Jeremiah 46:19–21

Once again *captivity,* or slavery was prophesied, this time by Jeremiah: ". . . furnish thyself to go into captivity . . ." Waste and desolate conditions are also prophesied for the city of Noph, ". . . for Noph shall be waste and desolate without an inhabitant." The Hebrew form 'Noph' is contracted from the ancient Egyptian common name Men-Nufr, known today as Memphis in Egypt. Noph is also called populous No' in Nahum 3:8. Noph was the capital and administrative center of Egypt about 3400 B.C.. In addition to being the seat of government, the city was also the center of worship of Ptah, the Egyptians' god of creation.

"The prophecy was fulfilled when the Persian Cambyses II took Memphis by siege in 525 B.C. and it began to decline in importance thereafter. This process was accelerated after the conquest of Egypt by Alexander the Great in 332 B.C. Ironically, the serious decay of the ancient city began after the rise of Christianity, when zealots of that faith defaced and destroyed the remaining pagan temples. In the 5th century A.D. the Christian monastery of Apa Jeremias rose among the tombs of Saqqara. The capital (Memphis) continued to deterioate, receiving its death blow during the Muslim conquest of Egypt in A.D. 640. Memphis was abandoned, and later the few remaining structures were dismantled so that the stone might be reused in the neighboring villages and in Cairo, after that city's foundation in the 10th century." (*Encyclopaedia Britannica,* 1983). ". . . for Noph (Memphis) shall be waste and desolate without an inhabitant."

Egypt, that lived in great pomp and plenty, not accustomed to the yoke of subjection, ". . . is like a very fair heifer . . .", a well-fed, fat and shining calf ready for the slaughter. Her 'hired men', (allied countries) shall fail her ". . . for they also are turned back, and are fled away together: they did not stand, because the day of their calamity was come upon them . . ."

> "The voice thereof shall go like a serpent; for they shall march with an army, and come against her with axes, as hewers of wood. They shall cut down her forest, saith the Lord, though it cannot be searched; because they are more than the grasshoppers, and are innumerable."

The Egyptians shall be no more able to resist the enemy than the tree is able to resist the man that comes with an axe to cut it down. Egypt, being very populous, was full of towns and cities, like a forest, and very rich, full of hidden treasures. The prophet predicts that Babylon shall make a great spoil in the land and shall overrun it as swarms of grasshoppers, for they are 'innumerable'.

> "The daughter of Egypt shall be confounded; *she shall be delivered into the hand of the people of the North.* The Lord of hosts, the God of Israel, saith Behold, I will punish the multitude of No (Noph) and Pharaoh, and Egypt, with their gods, and their kings; even Pharaoh, and all them that trust in him: And I will deliver them into the hand of those that seek their lives, and into the hand of Nebuchadnezzar king of Babylon, and into the hand of his servants: and afterward it shall be inhabited, as in the days of old, saith the Lord."—Jeremiah 46:24

'The daughter of Egypt' (translated the descendants of Egypt) shall be 'confounded'. The reason for their confusion shall be the fact that they are delivered into the 'hand of the people of the north'. In viewing a world map, the 'people of the north' are located directly north, just above the continent of Africa. They include the major countries of Europe: England, Germany Belgium, France, etc. The fulfillment of this portion of prophecy has been an enigma to native black Africans today who are confused and unable to understand why the Europeans (the people of the north) have been able to rule over their country for the past 300 years. ' The daughter (descendants) of Egypt shall be confounded (because) she shall be delivered into the hand of the people of the north.'

With the entrance of Nebuchadnezzar came also the beginning of much sorrow for the Egyptian people and their descendants. The Egyptians, who formerly carried war to the borders of other countries, now find to their great amazement that the alarm of war is sounded in their own land. But they shall not be successful for God has ordained their day of calamity: "Behold, I will punish . . . even Pharaoh, and all them that trust in him."

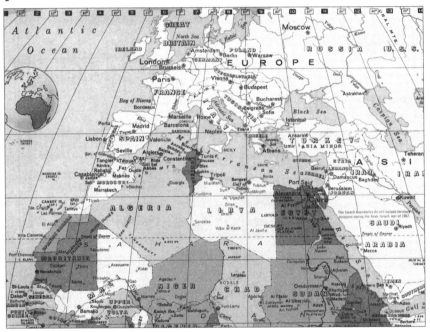

2 Kings 24:7 declares that after Egypt's defeat at Carchemish at the hands of Nebuchadnezzar, Egypt's kings never again made any other attempts upon other nations. "*And the King of Egypt came not again anymore out of his land: for the King of Babylon had taken from the river of Egypt unto the river Euphrates all that pertained to the King of Egypt.*"

"But fear not thou, O my servant Jacob, and be not dismayed O Israel: for behold I will save thee from afar off, and thy seed from the land of their captivity; and Jacob shall return, and be in rest and at ease, and none shall make him afraid. Fear thou not, O Jacob my servant, saith the Lord: for I am with thee: for I will make a full end of all the nations whither I have driven thee: but I will not make a full end of thee, but correct thee in measure; yet will I not leave thee wholly unpunished."—Jeremiah 46:27–28

God is merciful to the disobedient Jews who are yet dwelling in Egypt and promises to spare them: ". . . but I will not make a full end of thee, but *correct thee in measure: yet will I not leave thee wholly unpunished.*" On the other hand, the measure of Egypt's iniquity is too full and their end as a nation has come. They must now suffer the judgements of God. An intimation is given in verse 26 that in process of time Egypt shall recover itself again, 'And afterward it shall be inhabited, as in the days of old, saith the Lord.' However, as one finds in Ezekiel, they shall not be the same because God has sworn to make a 'full end' of Egypt: ". . . for I will make *a full end of all the nations whither I have driven thee.*" It is God's determination that Egypt shall never again be the nation that it once was.

Chapter 3

Ezekiel Chapters 29–32

The approximate length of time between the prophet Isaiah's message, which began about 713 B.C., and the prophet Jeremiah's message, which began about 586 B.C., is about 127 years. One year later, about the year 585 B.C., God sent Ezekiel with a message to the Egyptians, given at intervals over a period of about 14 years. It is commonly believed that the prophecies of Ezekiel are not written in their chronological order and the precise dates are not perfectly accurate.

As Ezekiel issues this last and final warning to Pharaoh, which consists of four chapters, it must be noted that this last message is longer in length than the messages delivered by the previous prophets, in an effort to persuade Pharaoh to change his mind and turn away from idolatry and sorcery. God is reluctant to execute final judgement upon the Egyptians, but in view of their continued disobedience, He could not continue to bless these people as a nation.

Ezekiel is the third and last prophet to appear before Pharaoh. All of them—Isaiah, Jeremiah and Ezekiel—appeared before Pharaohs at intervals over a period of approximately one hundred and forty-two years! At this point in time, when God sends Ezekiel, He knows that Egypt has hardened its heart to all the warnings and has chosen to continue on in their evil idolatrous ways. Therefore, the people were given over to idolatry and sorcery and to the worship of beasts, birds and natural forces. Consequently, when certain laws of the land are transgressed, evil forces begin to take over and the land itself will become defiled and undergo certain unnatural changes that will effect the environment; changes such as floods. deserts, famine and drought. "The earth also is defiled under the inhabitants thereof; *because* they have transgressed the laws, changed the ordinances, broken the everlasting covenant. Therefore hath the *curse* devoured the earth, and they that dwell therein are desolate." (Isaiah 24:5).

It is the belief of most people that Africa has always been rain forest, drought, famine, an overabundance of deserts, wild animals and illiterate natives running around naked and barefoot, knowing nothing but violence and voodoo. However, this is not the case. In the beginning everything God made was good, therefore, God did not create these disastrous conditions in the beginning. The state of Africa and its native descendants is the result of conditions that were allowed to befall the nation in the course of time, when man is left to himself and his own devices and allowed to wholly follow his own mind. It is a high price to pay for choosing to totally forsake the true God and to follow after other gods and beliefs.

As Ezekiel's prophecy is read, God cautions Pharaoh and Egypt that failure to heed the prophet's warning could result in even more losses and catastrophies for the nation: (1) And I will leave thee thrown into the wilderness (bush), (2) And the land of Egypt shall be desolate and waste (drought) (3) It shall be the basest of the kingdoms (the low esteem of the country today). The prophet also warns of the famous slave ships that would descend upon Africa. "In that day shall messengers go forth from me in *ships* to make the careless Ethiopians afraid, and great pain shall come upon them. as in the day of Egypt: for lo, it cometh." (Ezekiel 30:9). Other catastrophic conditions were prophesied, the consequences of which are discussed in detail.

In the latter portion of the 32nd chapter, God gives the prophet a command to relate a vision of what Pharaoh can expect when they die and their souls end up in hell! Yet, for all the pleading done, this Pharaoh hardened his heart, as all the other Pharaohs before him had done, and failed to heed the prophet's warning, setting in motion the sure word of God, with long-range effects that have afflicted the lives of black people from that day to this one!

74

"In the tenth year, in the tenth month, in the twelfth day of the month, the word of the Lord camre unto me saying, Son of man, set thy face against Pharaoh king of Egypt, *and prophesy against him, and against all Egypt*: Speak and say, Thus saith the Lord God; Behold, I am against thee, Pharaoh king of Egypt, the great dragon that lieth in the midst of his rivers, which hath said, *my river is mine own, and I have made it for myself*. But I will put hooks in thy jaws, and I will cause the fish of thy rivers to stick unto thy scales, *and I will bring thee up out of the midst of thy rivers*, and all the fish of thy rivers shall stick unto thy scales."—Ezekiel 29:1–4

The command to Ezekiel to 'set thy face against Pharaoh . . . and all Egypt' signifies that, all things considered, God has determined action against Egypt in view of nearly one hundred and twenty-seven years of warnings to the Pharaohs of that land. This king, who is believed to have been Pharaoh Hophra, is represented as a 'great dragon that lieth in the midst of his rivers' or one who dominates or rules over his domain. Hophra had reigned in great prosperity for 25 years and was so lifted up in pride over his success that it is said that his common boast was, 'not even a god could dispossess him of his power.' The 'great dragon . . . which hath said, My river is mine own, and I have made it for myself." The Nile is the longest river in the world, over 4,160 miles long. The Egyptians owed everything to the waters of the Nile River, it was the very heart and life of Egypt. Without the Nile Egypt would have been a desert, for no one could live in that sandy, rainless land. The melting snows and spring rains in the highlands far to the south swelled the upper river causing the Nile to overflow each year, dropping tons of rich, black earth in the Nile's valley. This happened, unfailingly, each year, thereby eliminating the fear of wearing out the soil, and as a result, Egypt always had bumper crops. Through the centuries, the Egyptians learned to help the river make the valley an oasis and to make the greatest possible use of the life-giving stream. Therefore, as the river was literally the sole source of fertitlity and wealth to Egypt, the kingdom was greatly enriched by the commerce afforded by the river. ". . . My river is mine own, and I have made it for myself . . ." It's very likely that this Pharaoh's attitude concerning the river and the prosperity it afforded the kingdom of Egypt, was the same absurd attitude held by the people themselves, displaying a contempt for the sovereignty of God.

The course God decides to take with this proud Pharaoh to humble him is to prophesy against his prosperity: ". . . I will put hooks in thy jaws . . . and I will bring thee up out of the midst of thy rivers, and all the fish of thy rivers shall stick unto thy scales." Not only would Hophra's successful reign soon be ended but it also spelled the end of Egypt's reign, ending thousands of years of sovereign rule. His servants, his soldiers, his people, Ethiopia and all of the land shall be drawn out with him for these shall 'stick to his scales' or adhere to their king, giving credence that the mind of the Pharaoh was also the mind of the Egyptian people. But all that 'stick to his scales' shall perish together with him, as fish cast upon dry ground.

> "And I will *leave thee thrown into the wilderness*, thee and all the fish of thy rivers: thou shalt fall upon the open fields; *thou shalt not be brought together, nor gathered: I have given thee for meat to the beasts of the field* and to the fowls of the heaven."—Ezekiel 29:5

This is the first mention of the wilderness or, fittingly put, the *bush*. The prophet decrees that God will remove them from civilization and everything that represents great success and intelligence and will cast them (thrown) into the *bush* (wilderness) signifying an uninhabited, isolated and desolate place. This portion of prophecy not only unveils the mystery of *why* the peoples of Africa are predominantly found in the bush, rural villages and rain forest country, but also accounts for *why* they are basically still in the bush today! "And I will *leave thee thrown into the wilderness, thee and all the fish of thy rivers.*" The translation of *leave*, according to *Vine's*, is in the sense of abandoning or forsaking.

Meaning, roughly paraphrased, that God cast them out of civilization, threw them into a desolate, deserted place and abandoned them there, or completely gave them over to do those things which were not convenient, (idol worship, sorcery, witchcraft, voodoo, hoodoo), leaving them thrown in the bush, never again to be recognized or restored again as a great and powerful nation. Imagine the disbelief in Pharaoh's mind as he listened to the prophet Ezekiel relate to him these calamities that were to come upon Egypt. Perhaps as he glanced around his fine palace, observing his immediate successes and prosperity, how he had improved the capabilities of the river, encouraging commerce with other nations and acquiring great wealth for Egypt, it surely must have been impossible for him to even begin to imagine that the great and powerful Egypt would one day end up in the bush, naked, barefoot and illiterate!

"And I will leave thee *thrown* into the wilderness . . . thou shalt fall upon the open fields . . ." The meaning for *thrown*, according to *Vine's*, is to cast or scatter: "I shall *scatter* you upon the open fields." African society today consists mainly of tribes (there are about 3,000!) and they are all scattered (thrown) in many different areas of the continent. Until a few years ago, there were tribes in Africa no man had ever seen and even today there are yet many wild and uncivilized places. For centuries there were rumours that a race of small black people existed somewhere in the heart of Africa. In 1863 P.B. Du Chaillu came upon them. In 1887, Stanley, while passing through a vast forest between the Congo and Lake Albert, found numbers of these little people, called Negrillos. Some were only three feet in height.

In 1980 two American missionaries, Jerry and Gail Rozell, first heard of the Vadoma tribe while on temporary leave in the U. S. to settle their private affairs and prepare to minister in Zimbabwe. These missionaries had it on "good authority" that somewhere out in the vast open plains of Zimbabwe were a tribe of very shy, two-toed Africans which legend called *The Ostrich People*, because

Abu Simbel. Two ancient temples of Ramses II.

they would all run and hide in the bush whenever anyone would approach their village. These people lived such secluded lives that many thought they were just a legend. No one believed in their existence until these two missionaries, through God's miraculous guidance, finally were able to locate them and give them the good news of the Gospel. (printed from *The Believer's Voice of Victory* magazine. vol. 11. No. 11. 1985. The Kenneth Copeland Ministries. Ft. Worth Texas)

A quote from Ali A. Mazrui: ". . . the interior of Africa had less interaction with external cultures than Europe and Asia experienced. Even interaction among African cultures themselves was considerably hampered by the absence in many societies of adequate means of travelling long distances. Many African societies lacked the wheel with which to make travelling wagons. Still others lacked the horse or comparable beast for long-distance travelling . . . The absence of both the wheel and the mobile beast of burden sentenced many African societies to *spatial isolation*.

Africa's limited capability for mobility continues to be a problem to the present day, but that is substantially because there was little prior development in the direction of increasing effective trade and cultural interaction among African peoples themselves."

". . . *Thou shalt fall upon the open fields; thou shalt not be brought together, nor gathered . . .*" The purpose of scattering the Egyptians throughout the wilderness was to prevent their ever coming together again as a people and a nation. It is for this reason that there are nearly 3,000 separate tribes in Africa and very few share a common language. There are from 800 to 1,000 different languages that are spoken in Africa! When God prophesied 'thou shalt not be brought together, nor gathered', He used the different languages to keep them apart, the same method He used in Genesis, when the whole earth was of one language and of one speech. As they commenced to build a City and a tower whose 'tower may reach unto heaven', (lest we be scattered abroad upon the face of the earth), God came down and intervened. "Go to, let us go down, and there confound (confuse) their language, that they may not understand one another's speech. So the Lord *scattered* them abroad from thence upon the face of all the earth . . ." (Thou shalt not be brought together).

The scattering or separation of the tribes, the spirit of disunity among the tribes and the language barrier were the primary reasons the European slave traders were able to so easily capture and enslave the Africans. Divided and scattered about in the bush, they could not come together as one nation and stand against the slavers, thereby preventing the kidnapping of so many millions. (Thou shalt not be brought together, *nor gathered*). The main task for many African countries today has been to devise forms of government that promote internal unity, as almost every African country is composed of different communities and ethnic groups that are sometimes hostile to one another. The inability to come together as one is the major factor that hinders the progress of the black people in South Africa, in addition to the hostility that yet exists among the tribes. In other places the language barrier compounds the problem, what with some 60,000,000 people who

79

speak more than 400 languages in West Africa alone! The Congo Basin is inhabited by many tribes speaking different languages, each tribe's language unique unto itself. The knowledge of most of the individual languages is still very inadequate and many have not yet been translated into writing. (Thou shalt not be brought together, nor gathered).

". . . I have given thee for meat to the beasts of the field and to the fowls of the heaven." The prophet also warns the Egyptians that the day is forthcoming when they would always have to be on the alert and beware of wild animals (I have given thee for meat to the beasts . . . and to the fowls . . .). In other words, they would be forced to protect themselves at all times from wild animals, lest they be destroyed. Well known is the fact that Africa is the home of the largest most ferocious animals in the world. In the beginning times of creation in order for the animals to be subdued, God placed fear of man in their hearts: "And the fear of you and the dread of you shall be upon every beast of the earth, and upon every fowl of the air, upon all that moveth upon the earth, and upon all the fishes of the sea; into your hand are they delivered. Every moving thing that liveth *shall be meat for you . . .*" (Genesis 9:2–3). Yet, concerning the Egyptians God determined "I have *given thee for meat to the beasts . . . and the fowls . . .*" There is among some of the animals in Africa an unnatural lack of fear for mankind. There are tribes that live in a group of huts arranged in a circle designed to protect them from wild animals. Yet, in spite of all precautions, there are occasions when certain animals have been known to attack and kill a sometimes careless tribesman. "I have given thee for meat to the beasts of the field and the fowls of the heaven." In other words, there would always be the danger of their being attacked by wild beasts and their flesh eaten up by the fowls of the air.

"And all the inhabitants of Egypt shall know that I am the Lord because they have been a staff of reed to the house of Israel. When they took hold of thee by thy hand, thou didst break, and render all their shoulder: and when they leaned upon thee, thou brakest, and madest all their loins to be at a stand. Therefore thus saith the Lord God; Behold, I will bring a sword upon thee, and cut off man and beast out of thee."—Ezekiel 29:6–8

Egypt shall no more be a leaning-post for the house of Israel neither for those Jews who chose to leave the land of Judah in order to dwell in Egypt. The Lord, in His jealousy over Israel, contends that the puny help that Egypt gave, in comparison to His, was, at best, as 'a staff of reed to the house of Israel, when they took hold of thee by thy hand, thou didst break . . . when they leaned upon thee, thou brakest . . .' He therefore determines, "Behold, I will bring a sword upon thee . . ." For Israel's sake too, Egypt's reign must end and their misleading guidance be terminated.

"And the land of Egypt shall be desolate and waste; and they shall know that I am the Lord: *because he hath said, the river is mine, and I have made it.* Behold, therefore, I am against thee, and against thy rivers, and *I will make the land of Egypt utterly waste and desolate, from the tower of Syene even unto the border of Ethiopia.*"— Ezekiel 29:9–10

Many of the chief cities that once made up 'the land of Egypt' now lay in ruins, desolate and waste. The great Memphis, once the capital of Ancient Egypt, never recovered from the Persian invasion under Cambyses II. Two small Arab villages and twenty pyramids, with the celebrated Sphinx, remain. The populous city of Thebes also served as capital and ruled over all Egypt in the era of its highest splendor. The city lies today a nest of Arab hovels amid crumbling columns and drifting sands. The Persian invader Cambyses, in 525 B.C., completed the destruction that the Babylonians had begun.

". . . And the land of Egypt shall be desolate and waste . . ." About one fourth of the land area of Africa is covered with thick tropical forest and bushland. Savannah, grassland which is called sudan, is open land with poor grass in some areas and trees are

Deserts cover about two-fifths of Africa. The great, bleak Sahara occupies much of northern Africa. It separates the Arab countries along the Mediterranean coast from the countries of central Africa. The shifting sand dunes and barren rocks of the Sahara form one of the most desolate areas in the world. Farmers can raise food only where there are oases or on the narrow strip of fertile land along the Nile River. Southern Africa has two smaller deserts.

Forests lie in the mountainous sections of eastern Africa and on the plateaus south of the Congo River. Evergreen forests grow in the extreme northern and southern parts of the continent. Tropical rain forests make up a coastal area along the Gulf of Guinea and a region along the equator. This region stretches from the gulf eastward to the eastern border of Congo (Leopoldville). All of Africa's forest regions together cover less than a fifth of the continent.

Grasslands cover more than two-fifths of the continent. Endless stretches of thick grasslands, called savannas, make up much of the southern half of Africa. Near the rain forests, the grass grows thick and tall, sometimes as high as 12 feet. Farther east, the savannas become dry bushlands, with wiry grass and thorny bushes. The grasslands form the heart of Africa. There live the farming and herding tribes that make up most of the newly independent nations.

widely scattered. Savannah covers about two-thirds of the country. Less than one quarter is good, cultivated farmland, covering only a small fraction of the continent. The Nile Valley, for example, is a green ribbon only about ten miles wide. The remainder is taken up by deserts. The continent is thinly settled in comparison to its size, about 17.1 people for every square mile of land, because very dry lands cannot support a large population.

". . . And they shall know that I am the Lord: becuase he hath said, the river is mine, and I have made it. Behold, therefore I am against thee, and against thy rivers . . ." The fulfillment of this prophecy developed in a most peculiar way. What with the immense drought condition that exists in Africa today, one would immediately think that the continent had a limited water supply. Such is not the case. With its many waterfalls, rivers and rapids, the continent has more than one third of all the potential water-power in the world! The Congo alone has about twenty percent of the world's water-power potential. Yet less than 5 percent of this power is being used. One reason is that the rivers are navigable only in sections because of the several rapids and deep gorges, a circumstance that contributes to the delay of development in Africa. For instance, in Angola, few Angolan rivers are navigable. The Kwanza can carry small craft upstream for about 140 miles. The Congo is navigable by ocean-going ships up to Noqui in Angola and to Matadi in Zaire. All Zaire-bound ships must use the Angolan territorial waters of the Congo River, which is not navigable at certain points inside-the Zaire territorial water limits.

Another factor is the incidence of bands of rock that have proved resistant to the erosive effect of the rivers' flow. According to scientific reasoning, tropical rivers generally do not carry large quantities of rock or stone; instead, they tend to carry loads of fine silt, produced by chemical weathering. "Behold, I am against thy rivers." Still another interesting reason is the fact that the water-falls are located in hard to reach areas and in regions where it would be very hard to develop industries. Victoria Falls, more than twice as wide and twice as deep as Niagara Falls, span the entire breadth of the Zambezi River. These waters have yet to be developed by dams or power plants. The little-known Lofoi River, in East Katanga Province of the Congo, sends its waters rushing down a cliff in the Kundelungu Mountains, making a sheer drop of an amazing 1,260 feet into the valley below. It is said to be the highest single-leap falls on the African continent, exceeded only by the 2,810 foot drop of the Tugela River Falls in Natal. An abundance of water exists in the rain-soaked river basins of the rain forests but some of these are unhealthy regions.

"Behold, I am against thy rivers." In other words, the abundance of waters available would no longer be easily accessible in the land as it once was, making it difficult for the inhabitants to avail themselves of it. For example, all of the important African rivers, including the famous Nile, are interrupted by cataracts, rapids and waterfalls. Science explains that the land movements caused ridges to be formed across the courses of the rivers. "Behold, I am against thy rivers."

". . . and I will make the land of Egypt utterly waste and desolate, from the tower of Syene even unto the border of Ethiopia." The Sahara is the largest tropical and climactic desert in the world. With an area of 3,320,000 square miles, it fills almost all of the east-west oriented northern part of the African continent and constitutes the western end of the Afro-Asian desert zone. According to the Encyclopaedia Britannica, although the desert is as large as the United States, it is estimated to contain barely 2,000,000 inhabitants. Huge areas, the size of some states in the U. S. are wholly empty, just as if a state the size of Utah or Montana were suddenly emptied of inhabitants. Encyclopaedia Britannica: ". . . wherever meager vegetation can support grazing animals or reliable water sources occur, scattered clusters of inhabitants have survived in fragile ecological balance with one of the harshest environments on earth." Most of the Sahara is just mile upon mile of hot, shifting sand dunes. There are also stretches of land that are hard and rocky. There is no part of the Sahara that does not get some rain (most of which is scanty) but as it falls through the air it evaporates before it strikes the ground. Only a narrow strip of fertile land along the Nile River and scattered places where palms and grasses grow, or oases, break up this vast desert land. ". . . and I will make the land of Egypt *utterly waste and desolate*, from the tower of Syene even unto the border of Ethiopia." Malnutrition in Africa is a major problem due to starvation caused by the long droughts in famine-plagued Ethiopia, and other countries: Gambia, Kenya, Senegal, Sierra Leone, Uganda, Zambia and many others. ". . . from the tower of Syene even unto the border of Ethiopia."

> "No foot of man shall pass through it, nor foot of beast shall pass through it, neither shall it be inhabited forty years. *And I will make the land of Egypt desolate in the midst of the countries that are desolate,* and her cities among the cities that are laid waste shall be desolate forty years: *and I will scatter the Egyptians among the nations, and will disperse them through the countries.* Yet thus saith the Lord God; *at the end of forty years will I gather the Egyptians from the people whither they were scattered.* And I will bring again the captivity of Egypt, *and will cause them to return into the land of Pathros,* into the land of their habitation; and *they shall be there a base kingdom. It shall be the basest of the kingdoms:* neither shall it exalt itself any more above the nations: *for I will diminish them, that they shall no more rule over the nations."*—Ezekiel 29:11

Thus far, the prophet has related the many paths the Egyptians' lives would take, for they are all delivered to many destinies that await them: some unto death and hell, some to the nether parts of the earth(scattered among the nations, dispersed among the countries), many would be left at the mercy of their conquerors, heralding in a future of hopelessness. As God declares, 'no foot of man shall pass through it (Egypt), nor foot of beast shall pass through it, neither shall it be inhabited forty years'. This decree forewarns that Egypt, for a period of time, shall be in a state of collapse. It is during this forty year period of time that Africa shall began to degenerate or retrogress, if you will. The environment and the climate shall be immensely effected, resulting in wilderness conditions better known to us as bush, rain forests, or jungles. Egypt shall be made "desolate in the midst of the countries that are desolate . . ." According to Dr. Leakey: "At just about the time that major developments in cultural evolution were taking place in Egypt, Syria, and Mesopotamia, the deserts became more extensive and then cut off Africa from the rest of the world, except for a narrow passageway down either side of the Nile River."

Uninhabited for forty years and heavily depopulated that "no foot of man . . . or beast . . . shall pass through it . . .", the landscape, utterly waste and desolate, shall become a snarling tangled up maze of thick forests, marshes, swamps, and bush.

Neither shall the land be heavily populated as it once was for God declares: ". . . and I will scatter the Egyptians among the nations, and will disperse them through the countries." This is the first scattering of the Egyptian people. "Yet thus saith the Lord God; At the end of forty years will I gather the Egyptians from the people whither they were scattered . . . and will cause them to return into the land of Pathros, into the land of their habitation . . ." It is into these changed environmental conditions, after forty years of being scattered among the nations, that God gathers them together again and cause them to return into their land, but not to the great and prosperous life they had once known. The land of their habitation shall no longer be the prosperous and thriving area situated on the Nile River, with easy access to the Mediterranean Sea and other civilizations. "I . . . will cause them *to return* into the land of Pathros." According to the *New Smith's Bible Dictionary*, *Pathros* is a term used to designate 'Upper Egypt.' The term *pathros* literally means "the southern land." Although scholars have debated the precise location of the pathros, they have all agreed to identify the area as Upper Egypt, the area known today as *Sub-Sahara*, all of the area located below the Sahara Desert, the southern land. Interestingly, the major jungle conditions of Africa are located in Sub-Sahara Africa. "I will *cause* them to return into the land of Pathros . . ." From the book *Man in Africa*: "Very gradually, as the region continued to dry up, the game herds retreated into the tropical forests *farther south, and so did the people*." According to Dr. Leakey's account: "As the Sahara, which is located directly north in Africa, began to dry up, it virtually cut the African people off from the rest of the world. All of the area *below the Sahara (Sub-Sahara)* was totally cut off except for the narrow passageway down either bank of the Nile River. Africa could not be reached except to cross the Sahara Desert, *which acted as a deterrent*. Further south the narrow passageway formed by the Nile was completely closed by the swamps of what is called The Sudd.

From that time on, most of Africa became virtually isolated . . . *it was then that Africa lost its position as the leading continent in the world*. Up until this time, nearly every important and significant step in the development of man had taken place in Africa but now, Africa ceased to play the dominant role in world progress, after having led for . . . thousands of years."

Today the native black Africans are basically located in Sub-Sahara Africa, all of the area south of the Sahara Desert. ". . . I will cause them to *return* into the land of Pathros . . ." In other words, the Lord was returning the Egyptians back to the place they had originally started from Pathros, the southern land, better known as Upper Egypt, known today as Sub-Sahara Africa. All the way back to the place of the predynastic Egyptians who laid the foundation for the civilization of Ancient Egypt thousands of years before the Pharaohs. As a matter of fact, important finds in the Nile Valley prove that a dark-skinned people were the major benefactors of the famous civilization known today as Ancient Egypt, long before the pyramids of the Pharaohs. Herodotus the Greek writer, was much criticized for his theory that the early predynastic Egyptians were

African. However, at the beginning of the nineteenth century, Dr. R.R. Madden made a special study of skulls of different Eastern races. In Upper Egypt he saw several thousand mummy heads and he opened the heads of fifty mummies; they were all extremely narrow across the forehead and oblong in shape, like the heads of Nubians in measurement rather than like those of Copts. Herodotus was correct; the original predynastic people of Upper Egypt were of essentially African stock, *a character always retained despite alien influence brought to bear on them from time to time.* " Man gradually pushed *northwards* and that man", wrote Herodotus, "was African".

Upon being returned to Pathros (Sub-Sahara Africa), Africa began to become known as 'The Dark Continent'. Apparently, God literally used the Sahara Desert as a deterrent and a barrier to eliminate any more contact with civilization because He had ordained, ". . . and they shall be *there* (Sub-Sahara) a base kingdom. It shall be the *basest of the kingdoms: neither shall it exalt itself any more above the nations: for I will diminish them, that they shall no more rule over the nations.*" Africa is, even to this day, looked upon as the basest of kingdoms (nations). The word *base*, according to *Vine's*, denotes that which is of no reputation or fame in the world's esteem, that which is low and does not rise far from the ground. Casual reference to the continent of Africa is almost always to point out the backwardness and basic ignorance of its native black people, making it very hard to believe that these are the descendants of a people that ruled over and was exalted above other nations, "neither shall it exalt itself any more above the nations . . ." By the Almighty God's own admission Egypt was exalted and acclaimed above the other nations. He prophesies, however, that Egypt shall never be the same again, "for I will diminish them, that they shall *no more* rule over the nations." The word *diminish* means primarily a lessening, to make inferior, a decrease or a loss, meaning a national diminution or diminishing. According to Lerone Bennett Jr. history records this period of diminishing as "A time that Africa was in a state of unstable equilibrium.

The continent had emerged from the 'Golden Age of the Great Empires' with a number of critical problems, including climactic changes which pushed the Sahara south, triggering massive migrations and isolating large sections from the dominant currents of the age." These events would change Europe and Africa forever because according to Bennett: "Europe's eminence one must remember, came in large part *after* the fall of Africa and as a direct result of that fall."

> "And it shall be no more the confidence of the house of Israel. which bringeth their iniquity to remembrance, when they shall look after them: but they shall know that I am the Lord God."—Ezekiel 29:16

God, who by His own divine admission, is a jealous God, makes it very plain that He is jealous over the confidence that the children of Israel placed in the Egyptians. His intent is that Israel as well as Egypt should know, without a doubt, ". . . that I am the Lord God."

> "And it came to pass in the seven and twentieth year, in the first month, in the first day of the month, the word of the Lord came unto me saying, Son of man, Nebuchadnezzar king of Babylon caused his army to serve a great service against Tyrus: every head was made bald, and every shoulder was peeled: yet had he no wages, nor his army, for Tyrus, for the service that he had served against it: Therefore thus saith the Lord God; Behold, I will give the land of Egypt unto Nebuchadnezzar king of Babylon; and he shall take her multitude, and take her spoil, and take her prey; and it shall be the wages for his army. I have given him the land of Egypt for his labour wherewith he served against it, *because they wrought for me*, saith the Lord God. In that day will I cause the horn of the house of Israel to bud forth, and I will give thee the opening of the mouth in the midst of them; and they shall know that I am the Lord."—Ezekiel 29:17–21

It is generally believed, historically, that Nebuchadnezzar's invasion and conquest of Egypt did not take place until after the conquest of the great city of Tyre. Nebuchadnezzar spent thirteen years in the siege of Tyre. Although there are no records of the actual circumstances concerning the conquest, however, it is probable that the Tyrians, before they surrendered their city, managed to remove much of their treasure, therefore Nebuchadnezzar's army reaped very little for "the service that he had served against it." During all that time, the Egyptians were at war with the Cyrenians, by which they were much weakened and impoverished. At the end of the siege of Tyre, Nebuchadnezzar's army had suffered immensely, "every head was bald, and every shoulder peeled", with carrying burdens and labouring. For their services they had no wages, for the Tyrians had sent away by ship their best effects, and threw the rest into the sea, so that there was nothing but bare walls. For that reason God declared, "Behold, I will give the land of Egypt unto Nebuchadnezzar "and he shall take her multitude, and take her spoil, and take her prey; and it shall be the wages for his army. I have given him the land of Egypt for his labour wherewith he served against it. because they wrought (worked) for me, saith the Lord God." The possession of Egypt became Nebuchadnezzar's reward.

> "The word of the Lord came again unto me saying, Son of man, prophesy and say, Thus saith the Lord God; Howl ye, Woe worth the day! For the day is near, even the day of the Lord is near, a cloudy day; it shall be the time of the heathen. And the sword shall come upon Egypt, and great pain shall be in Ethiopia, when the slain shall fall in Egypt, and they shall take away her multitude, and her foundations shall be broken down. Ethiopia, Libya, and Lydia, and all the mingled people, and Chub, and the men of the land that is in league, shall fall with them by the sword. Thus saith the Lord; They also that uphold Egypt shall fall; and the pride of her power shall come down: from the tower of Syene shall they fall in it by the sword, saith the Lord God."—Ezekiel 30:1–6

The historic period of Egyptian history is called the Dynastic Period—the time covered between the first Dynasty and the Ptolemaic Period. The early Dynastic Period (3100–2686) began with the uniting of Upper and Lower Egypt. Unification was the most important event in the country's existence; so important that almost immediately Egyptian civilization began to manifest and reveal great creative forces that were to remain trademarks of the Egyptians for thousands of years. Their independent creativeness made them the outstanding leaders of the Ancient World with important discoveries and inventions that led to the founding of civilization as we know it today. In Herodotus' writings, his picture of Egypt as an unchanging civilization became the image of Egypt to succeeding generations; "The Egyptians", he wrote, "adhere to their own national customs and adopt no foreign usages".

The physical nature of Egypt rendered it difficult to rule, even under the most favorable conditions, the land being 500 miles in length but scarcely any breadth. Possibly, for that reason, all the important high officials, known as princes, fulfilled their national and provincial duties at the royal residence, or capital city. The princes' responsibilities stemmed directly from the king, and they were answerable only to him. This practice started with the Egyptians. A king who delegated power to the local officials in the provinces was simply courting disaster, therefore, they administered their duties in the presence of the king where they could be observed and prevented from becoming too powerful. This closely centralized form of government provided the great strength and foundation of Egypt. However, the prophet warns: ". . . the sword shall come upon Egypt, and great pain shall be in Ethiopia, when the slain shall fall in Egypt, and they shall take away her multitude and her foundations shall be broken down." "The pride of her power shall come down."

Neighboring states in alliance with Egypt, as Ethiopia, Libya, Lydia, all the mingled people (foreigners who settled in Egypt), Chub (some tribe in alliance with Egypt), and the men of the land, shall fall with them by the sword.

"And they shall be desolate in the midst of the countries that are desolate, and her cities shall be in the midst of the cities that are wasted. And they shall know that I am the Lord, when I have set a fire in Egypt and when all her helpers shall be destroyed."—Ezekiel 30:7-8

At Thebes, the most magnificent city in all Egypt, the temple ruins of Karnak and Luxor testify to the great pains that were taken to make them beautiful. Nothing remains of the royal city of Memphis but the ruins of temples, palaces and dwellings. Whole cities, to say nothing of tablets, tombs and artifacts, have been dug out of Egyptian soil in this century. More untapped discoveries surely lie waiting for modern science to find a way to reach them. "And they shall be desolate in the midst of the countries that are desolate, and her cities shall be in the midst of the cities that are wasted."

"In that day shall messengers go forth from me *in ships* to make the careless Ethiopians afraid, *and great pain shall come upon them*, as in the day of Egypt: for lo, it cometh."—Ezekiel 30:9

This is the first mention of the well-known and famous slave ships. Lerone Bennett, Jr. (*Before the Mayflower—A History of Black America*) relates it this way: "The newly-purchased slaves, properly branded and chained, were then rowed out to the slave ships for the dreaded Middle Passage across the Atlantic. They were packed like books on shelves into holds, which in some instances were no higher than eighteen inches. 'They had not so much room.' one captain said, 'as a man in his coffin, either in length or breadth. It was impossible for them to turn or shift with any degree of ease.' Here, for the six to ten weeks of the voyage, the slaves lived like animals. Under the best conditions, the trip was intolerable. When epidemics of dysentry or smallpox swept the ships, the trip was beyond endurance.

'On many of these ships', a contemporary said, 'the sense of misery and suffocation was so terrible in the 'tween-decks where the height sometimes was only eighteen inches, so that the unfortunate slaves could not turn round, were wedged immovably, in fact, and chained to the deck by the neck and legs that the slaves not infrequently would go mad before dying or suffocating. In their frenzy some killed others in the hope of procuring more room to breathe. Men strangled those next to them, and women drove nails into each other's brains.' It was common, John Newton said, to find a dead slave and a living slave chained together. So many dead people were thrown overboard on slavers that it was said that sharks picked up ships off the coast of Africa and followed them to America. *"In that day shall messengers go forth from me in ships . . . and great pain shall come upon them . . . for lo, it cometh."*

> "Thus saith the Lord God; I will also make the multitude of Egypt to cease by the hand of Nebuchadnezzar king of Babylon. He and his people with him, the terrible of the nations shall be brought to destroy the land: and they shall draw their swords against Egypt, and fill the land with the slain."—Ezekiel 30:10–11

It shall be the day of destruction for Egypt and all the states and countries in confederacy with her. "I will also make the multitude of Egypt to cease . . ." That populous country shall be depopulated, for many shall fall by the sword, even from the tower of Syene, which is in the utmost corner of the land. The Egyptians have had their day, now God shall have His day, the day of the revelation of His righteous judgement.

> "And I will make the rivers dry, and *sell the land into the hand of the wicked*: and I will *make the land waste*, and all that is therein, *by the hand of strangers*: I the Lord have spoken it."—Ezekiel 30:12

This portion of prophecy is very moving in its fulfillment, as we shall see. The invasion of the Babylonians and the conquest of

Egypt by Nebuchadnezzar marked the beginning of sorrows and pain for the Egyptians. The land would never again be the same as it was before for there would be a continuous train of invaders and foreigners in the land of Africa. Mediterranean or Northern Africa, the only part of the continent that was well-known to Asia and Europe, was first colonized by Phoenicians between 1100–800 B.C. on the coast of what is today known as Tunisia. North Africa was the first part of the continent to be taken over by foreigners. In 332 B.C. Alexander the Great founded the city of Alexandria in Egypt. Rome conquered Carthage in 146 B.C. and by the year 114 A.D. all of North Africa, from the Atlantic Ocean to the Red Sea, including Egypt, was part of the Roman Empire until 640 A.D. Between 640 and 646 A.D. the Arabs conquered Egypt and took possession of all of North Africa. These invasions carried the Arabs across the Sahara to the south, and close links were developed between North Africa and Africa south of the Sahara. These links, however, did not go beyond the northern fringes of the tropical rain forests, where impenetrable jungles and unknown dangers halted the advance of the Arabs. Therefore, the Arabs are found basically in the northern part of Africa. Although the entire coastline of Africa was known to most of the world, much of its interior remained a mystery. About the year 1517 North Africa fell into the hands of the strongest of the Mohammedan people, the Ottoman Turks. The Turks' control of Egypt continued without interruption until Napoleon's invasion of the country in 1798. Somewhere in the 1400s the Portuguese established settlements on the west coast and the knowledge of the wealth that could be obtained in that region attracted traders, colonizers, and explorers from England, Spain, Holland, France, and Denmark to Africa. In 1879 King Leopold II of Belgium sent Stanley to get the Congo region for him. This started a race for African lands.

"And I will . . . sell the land into the hand of the wicked . . ." It is during this period in history that the prophecy to "sell the land into the hand of the wicked" began to be manifested. The world was created with incredible wealth and Africa has a very large share of the world's mineral resources. Often referred to as "God's Treasure Chest", Africa's known mineral wealth makes it the world's richest continent. From the years of contact with the coast of Africa the Europeans knew that raw materials needed for their industries were easily accessible, numerous and easily obtainable in Africa. From the beginning of the 16th century to the last quarter of the 19th, Africa was explored and colonized, mainly by Great Britain, France, Portugal, Holland, Spain, Italy, Belgium and Germany. All the European countries sent out explorers and during this period they subdued many African tribes. By 1884, the intense rivalry and the frequent disputes between the European powers over African territory threatened the stability of international relations. In view of the situation, King Leopold II of Belgium, taking the initiative, called a conference at Berlin of 14 powerful countries (including the United States) to settle the partitioning of Africa. The Berlin Conference was Africa's undoing in more than one way. When the conference convened in Berlin, over 80 percent of Africa was still under traditional African rule, but the colonial powers, nevertheless, superimposed their boundary lines on the African continent, haggling over pieces of territory, erasing and redrawing boundaries through known as well as unknown regions, as if no humans existed on the continent. African peoples were divided, unified regions were ripped apart, hostile societies were thrown together, migration routes were closed off. Such was the effect when the colonial powers began to consolidate their holdings. "And I will . . . *sell the land into the hand of the wicked . . .*"

When the rush was over, only the Christian nation of ancient Ethiopia and the Republic of Liberia were still independent. The rest of the great continent was parceled out and separated among the European powers. The aftermath is a permanent liability upon the geographical map of Africa resulting from three months of

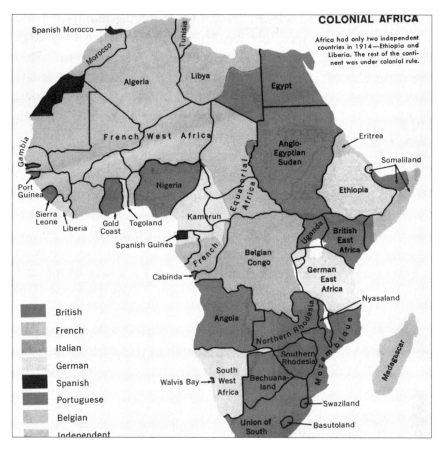

COLONIAL AFRICA

Africa had only two independent countries in 1914—Ethiopia and Liberia. The rest of the continent was under colonial rule.

Legend:
- British
- French
- Italian
- German
- Spanish
- Portuguese
- Belgian
- Independent

Map labels: Spanish Morocco, Tunisia, Morocco, Algeria, Libya, Egypt, French West Africa, Eritrea, Somaliland, Gambia, Port Guinea, Nigeria, Equatorial Africa, Anglo-Egyptian Sudan, Ethiopia, Sierra Leone, Liberia, Gold Coast, Togoland, Kamerun, Spanish Guinea, French, Belgian Congo, Uganda, British East Africa, German East Africa, Nyasaland, Cabinda, Angola, Northern Rhodesia, Mozambique, Madagascar, Southern Rhodesia, South West Africa, Walvis Bay, Bechuanaland, Swaziland, Union of South, Basutoland

ignorant, greedy acquisitiveness during Europe's insatiable search for minerals and markets. After the Berlin Conference of 1885, during which rules for the competition over African lands were laid down, each country taking over enormous sections of Africa's continent, annexing as much land as they could, wherever they could—exploitation of the continent began in earnest and the age of colonialism in Africa began to seriously get underway. The Europeans, in order to be able to stake their claims properly, needed to know more about Africa: its geography, its natural resources and the friendliness or hostility of its people. Having no knowledge of guns and rifles, the Africans fell easy prey to the armies of Europe. Explorers began to move into the interior of Africa:

96

David Livingstone, Herbert Stanley, Mungo Park, Richard Burton, Heinrich Barth Speke, Rene Caillie, Paul Soleillet and others. Africa was at the mercy of adventurers, prospectors, traders, concessionaries, and fortune hunters who were attracted to it. These were followed by chartered companies, corporations and syndicates, followed by European governments and so-called "protectorates" which soon developed into colonies and overseas provinces. Arguing that the Europeans were bringing the wealth of technology, Christianity and education to a people desperately in need of them, private companies, financed at no cost to the taxpayers, would sometimes undertake the colonization of an area so that their government could not control the details of their operations.

In 1880, 90 percent of Africa was ruled by Africans. By the beginning of the 20th century, a mere 20 years later, the whole of Africa, except Ethiopia and Liberia, was wholly under European colonial rule, being used and regarded solely as a highly potential source of raw materials as well as a natural market for Europe. By 1912 95 percent of Africa had been divided among the European nations and was to remain so until after World War II, when the era of African independence began to emerge. "And I will . . . *sell the land into the hand of the wicked . . .*"

The *1989 World Almanac and Book of Facts* gives this account of an article that was published between the years of 1880–1900:

> **"Imperialism Triumph.** The vast African interior, visited by European explorers (Barth, 1821–65, Livingstone, in 1813-73) was conquered by the European powers in rapid, competitive thrusts from their coastal bases after 1880, mostly for domestic political and international strategic reasons. West African Moslem kingdoms (Fulani) Arab slave traders (Zanzibar) and Bantu military confederations (Zulu) *were alike subdued. Only christian Ethiopia and Liberia resisted successfully.* France (West Africa) and Britain (Cape to Cairo) were the major beneficiaries. The ideology of "The White Man's Burden" of a "civilizing mission" . . . *justified the conquests.*"

"And I will . . . *sell the land into the hand of the wicked . . .*"

". . . *And I will make the land waste, and all that is therein, by the hand of strangers . . .*" *Vine's Expository Dictionary* defines "waste" as destruction, squandering property, to ravage, destroy, maltreat or make havock of. The partitioning of Africa's continent resulted in long-lasting effects, proving harmful to Africa's land as well as its economic development. With no regard for the native people, these European countries began to freely avail themselves, laying claim to the very soil of the land itself, with all its valuable wealth and resources. The vast riches of Africa are so great that many White men, over the past 300 years, have braved the heat, disease and perilously dangerous conditions to pursue them. In 1965, jungle conditions made it very difficult for mahogany and other rare and expensive hardwoods to be cut down because of the abundance of mosquitoes, the tsetse fly that causes sleeping sickness, termites, cobras, puff adders, vipers, and giant scorpions. Nevertheless, in spite of these hazards, tractors, bulldozers, dynamite and construction companies daily tear up the virgin soil in search of wealth in the land of Africa. With no consideration for preservation of the land, trees are cut indiscriminately with no particular concern for conservation. No thought of protection, care or control is employed. "*I will make the land waste, and all that is therein, by the hand of strangers.*"

Some would argue that the Europeans brought in much-needed technology and skills. "But", argues Ali A. Mazrui, "It is only a mirage, a facade. Europeans have brought Western technology into Africa only to leave behind various forms of waste and desolation." Several of the last remaining European colonies were granted independence in the years 1976 and 1977 and their governments were taken over by the native Africans. The Europeans who did not choose to make Africa their home any longer, simply decided to shut down their corporations, with no regard for their black employees, leaving buildings and factories either deserted or no longer in use refusing to help to develop Africa for the benefit of Africa herself. "*I will make the land waste, and all that is therein, by the hand of strangers.*"

> "Thus saith the Lord God; I will also destroy the idols, and I will cause their images to cease out of Noph; and *there shall be no more a prince of the land of Egypt*: and I will put a fear in the land of Egypt."—Ezekiel 30:13

Noph, better known as Memphis, Egypt, was metropolis and capital of Lower Egypt and remained important even after the capital was transferred to Thebes and until Alexandria was established. The Hebrews called it Noph. It never recovered from the ravages of Cambyses II in the year 525 B.C. "I will . . . destroy the idols . . . will cause their images to cease out of Noph."

It is almost impossible to express the degree of confidence that the Ancient Egyptians placed in their idols and gods, a confidence that was also shared by other nations. Moses' father-in-law, Jethro, was the priest and chief of a clan called Kenites, part of the tribe of Midianites who wandered the desert areas of the northern Sinai peninsula. Exodus 18:10–11 relates how Jethro rejoiced exceedingly upon receiving the news that God had delivered the Israelites out of the hand of the Egyptians. "And Jethro said, Blessed be the Lord, who hath delivered you out of the hand of the Egyptians, and out of the hand of Pharaoh, who hath delivered the people from under the hand of the Egyptians. *Now I know that the Lord is greater than all Gods: for in the thing wherein they dealt proudly*, he was above them." Notice the amazement in his expression (*now I know*) over the wonder of God's ability to excel over the power of the Egyptians' gods because their faith in the powers of their gods was the thing wherein they were the most proud. However, God determines to "destroy the idols . . . and . . . cause their images to cease . . ."

It has been said that, "All things dread Time, but Time itself dreads the Pyramids." Although today these magnificent structures

In Egypt, the "Fallen Colossus" of Luxor.

Ruins of Thebes, a famous old Egyptian city, which stood on the site of the modern town of Karnak. The two pointed shafts shown at the left and right of the picture are obelisks—monuments representing the sun-god, Ra.

are battered and broken, they have not entirely lost their magnificence. The temple of Ammon, the largest and most splendid, took almost 400 years to build. One can only marvel at the genius of the ancient architects and wonder how it came to be built in an age long before high-tech machinery was known. Very wonderful too are the temple of the moongod Khensu and the temple of Ramses III. The doorways of the temple of Amenhotep III was studded with gold and the forecourt was paved with silver. However, because of the sin of idolatry connected with these wondrous works, God declared destruction upon them. Massive colonades are about all that remain of the temples. The gigantic statues of Ramses II lie toppled over on the ground.

It's interesting to note that as a tribute to the genius of the Ancient Egyptian architects, during the early 1960s worldwide efforts were made to rescue certain archaeological monuments that were threatened by the rising waters of Lake Nasser , behind the Aswan High Dam on the upper Nile River. Fifty governments raised $36,000,000 to save the temples of Ramses II and his wife, Nefertari at Abu Simbel. The statues and columns were cut into 30-ton blocks, hoisted 200 feet to the top of the cliff and there they were reassembled. However, it is reported that the engineers were unable, with all of their modern-day technology, to reassemble every detail of the monuments exactly the way the Egyptians had originally built them.

Reconstitution of the fantastic appearance of the temple of Abu-Simbel.

". . . And there shall be no more a *prince* of the land of Egypt . . ." 'Prince, of course, meaning Pharaoh'. In 605 B.C., as we recall, when Pharaoh-Necho was defeated in battle by Nebuchadnezzar, Apries, a later Pharaoh of the dynasty, was deposed about 569 B.C. by Ahmose II, who withstood attacks by both the Babylonians

102

and the Persians. In 525 B.C., however, his son and successor Psamtik III was conquered by Cambyses II king of Persia. With this defeat, the kingdom totally collapsed, bringing to a close Egyptian rule. Psamtik III was the last native Egyptian Pharaoh. From that time to this day, upwards of 2,000 years ago, no native Egyptian Pharaoh ever ruled anymore over Africa.

However, the glory surrounding the image of 'Pharaoh of Egypt' carried with it a magnificence that was not so easily cast

Khafre, Egyptian King and pyramid-builder in the Fourth Dynasty, 2900–2750 B.C. The power of a great rule is expressed in this rigid figure, carved from the hardest stone.

aside. In 305 B.C., after receiving the governship of Egypt, Ptolemy I, a Macedonian, established Egypt as an independent monarchy, taking the title of 'Pharaoh'. This state of affairs continued and the kingdom flourished for nearly 200 years under the

Ptolemies until the deaths in 30 B.C. of the last of the Ptolemaic line, the famous Cleopatra.

Ramses the Great

"... *and I will put a fear in the land of Egypt.*" Obviously, there was no faintheartedness or timidity in the character of the Egyptian people. The bravery and courage of her men of war was her support, the kind of courage that could appreciate a danger and steadfastly face it. This quality of mind or temperament enabled them to stand fast in the face of opposition and danger. This quality shall no longer be a stronghold for Egypt for God has declared: "I will put a fear in the land of Egypt." A spirit of fear shall dominate the land, a fear that will penetrate the very hearts and minds of the Egyptians, destroying a legend of dauntless courage that had endured for thousands of years.

> "And I will make Pathros desolate, and will set fire in Zoan, and will execute judgements in No. And I will pour my fury upon Sin, the strength of Egypt; and I will cut off the multitude of No. And I will set fire in Egypt: Sin shall have great pain, and No shall be rent asunder, and Noph shall have distresses daily. The young men of Aven and of Pibeseth shall fall by the sword: and these cities shall go into captivity.
>
> At Tahpanhes also the day shall be darkened, when I shall break there the yokes of Egypt: and the pomp of her strength shall cease in her: as for her, a cloud shall cover her, and her daughters shall go into captivity. Thus shall I execute judgements in Egypt: and they shall know that I am the Lord."—Ezekiel 30: 14–19

No place in the land of Egypt shall be exempted from the fury of the wrath of God, not the strongest nor the remotest. Various places are named: Pathros, Zoan, the city of No, Sin, Noph, Aven, Pi-Beseth and Tahpanhes. God chose to put these primary cities of sin completely out of commission by destroying them. The destructions named carry with them lasting effects: their multitude shall be cut off, they shall have great pain and be rent asunder with daily distresses. Their day shall be darkened (hopes extinguished). Their young men shall die by the sword and in addition, their daughters (descendants) shall go into captivity (slavery).

These principal cities of sin had the same type of effect upon the land of Egypt as California and New York have upon the United States of America. Every type of practice that originated in these cities, whether good or bad, was sure to spread all over the land. Therefore, the Lord determined "I shall *break the yokes of Egypt*", meaning that Egypt's strong influence over the land shall be spoiled or broken that they shall no more reign supreme. "And the pomp of her strength shall cease in her . . ." The show or display (pomp) of their national supremity and power, the multitude of people, their great armies, horses and mighty chariots, and fantastic abilities in areas of science, astrology, shall be cut off ". . . shall cease in her . . ."

". . . as for her, a cloud shall cover her . . ." or a shadow that will dim their hopes as well as their glory. "Thus will I execute judgements in Egypt . . ." The execution of these judgements spelled the absolute end of a culture, a civilization and a people that would never again play a major role in world affairs. "And they shall know that I am the Lord."

> "And it came to pass in the eleventh year, in the first month, in the seventh day of the month, that the word of the Lord came unto me saying, Son of man, I have broken the arm of Pharaoh king of Egypt; and lo, it shall not be bound up to be healed, to put a roller to bind it, to make it strong to hold the sword. Therefore thus saith the Lord God; Behold, I am against Pharaoh king of Egypt, and will break his arms, the strong, and that which was broken; and I will cause the sword to fall out of his hand."—Ezekiel 30:20

It is three months later that the prophet approaches Pharaoh with yet another warning from the Lord: "Behold, I am against thee and have broken thy arms (strength and power) that you shall never again be victorious in battle." When God determines to break the power of a nation, there is nothing that nation can do to restore it or renew it, ". . . and lo, it shall not be bound up to be healed, to put a roller to bind it (a bandage), to make it strong to hold the sword." There is no power given to a nation but what is given from above. This divine action marked the point at which God ordained that Egypt shall never again be strong enough to defend itself against foreign invaders, a fact that is yet true even to this day.

"And I will *scatter the Egyptians among the nations*, and will disperse them through the countries."—Ezekiel 30:23

As early as the 1500s Africans were brought into the West Indies, Central America, Latin America. South America, Haiti and Mexico. In 1619 about 18–20 Africans were brought to the Virginia colony so that some present-day Blacks probably have an older heritage in America than do the descendants of the Pilgrims who came on the Mayflower. In 1650 the continent of Africa had nearly a fifth of the world's population. For almost 290 years thereafter, Africa was raided continuously by slave traders being literally 'scattered . . . among the nations . . . and dispersed through the countries: Europe, Arabia, Turkey, Persia, India, North America, Panama, Peru, Caribbean, Brazil and other parts.

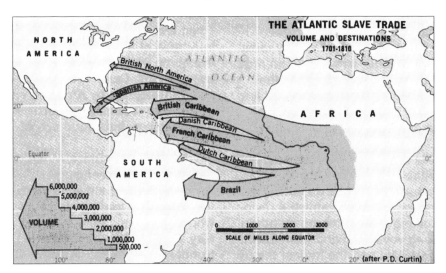

Lerone Bennett Jr. states: "The human factories in Africa struggled to keep up with the demand. In the eighteenth century between fifty thousand and one hundred thousand slaves crossed the Atlantic each year. The greatest number, by far, went to the West Indies and Brazil. At least two million were shipped to the West Indies. Joao Pandia Calogeras, the Brazilian historian, said at least eighteen million were shipped to Brazil. Arthur Ramos,

107

another Brazilian, thinks this figure is too high. Five million, he says, is a more accurate figure.

Large blocks of slaves were dropped off in Spanish colonies in the Caribbean and in Central and South America. As early as 1553 there were 20,000 Blacks in Mexico. Some 200,000 slaves were imported before slavery was abolished in Mexico in the first quarter of the nineteenth century. Hundred of thousands of slaves were scattered over the areas of present-day Panama, Colombia, Ecuador, Chile, Peru, and Venezuela. *"And I will scatter the Egyptians among the nations, and will disperse them through the countries."*

> "And I will strengthen the arms of the king of Babylon, and put my sword in his hand: but I will break Pharaoh's arms and he shall groan before him with the groanings of a deadly wounded man. But I will strengthen the arms of the king of Babylon, and the arms of Pharaoh shall fall down; and they shall know that I am the Lord, when I shall put my sword into the hand of the king of Babylon, and he shall stretch it out upon the land of Egypt."— Ezekiel 30:24–25

Clearly, God Almighty ordained the descension of the Egyptian nation, causing them to decline in world power, superiority, wealth, authority, recognition, population and prosperity. It is at this time that God began to elevate other nations over the nation of Egypt. One of Pharaoh's arms had already been broken due to Egypt's terrible defeat at Carchemish at the hands of Nebuchadnezzar a fatal blow from which Egypt never fully recovered. As Egypt decreased, the other nations increased beginning with Babylon who had but lately arrived at its station of great pomp and power, after God had given Nebuchadnezzar the victory over the great kingdom of Assyria followed by Alexander the Great, Rome and all the other nationalities that came after.

"I will strengthen the arms of the king of Babylon . . ." The kingdom of Egypt was very ancient and had been a nation of people to be reckoned with for literally thousands of years. However,

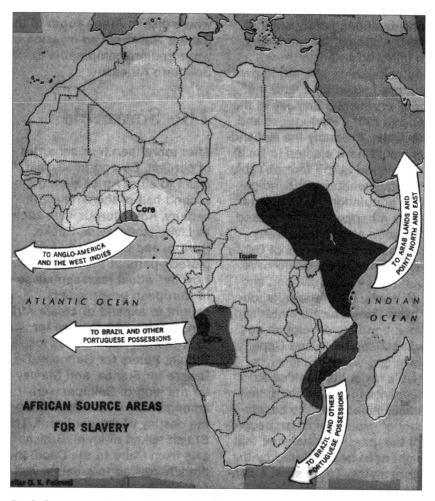

Core

TO ANGLO-AMERICA
AND THE WEST INDIES

TO ARAB LANDS AND
POINTS NORTH AND EAST

ATLANTIC OCEAN

Equator

INDIAN
OCEAN

TO BRAZIL AND OTHER
PORTUGUESE POSSESSIONS

AFRICAN SOURCE AREAS
FOR SLAVERY

TO BRAZIL AND OTHER
PORTUGUESE POSSESSIONS

After D. K. Fieldhouse

God determined that Egypt shall grow weaker and Babylon shall grow stronger, edging out a people, a civilization, a culture, the like of which has yet to be equalled. ". . . I will strenghthen the arms of the king of Babylon . . . but I will break Pharaoh's arms . . . and the arms of Pharaoh shall fall down . . ." This decision was not based on the inferiority of the Egyptians but, on the contrary, it was partly the Egyptians' confidence in their own superiority that got them in trouble with God, thereby prompting His decision to diminish them.

"And they shall know that I am the Lord, when I shall put

'My Sword' into the hand of the king of Babylon . . ." Using the term 'my sword' the Lord indicates, in no uncertain terms, that it is He who gives the power and ability to excell in battle, signifying that it is through His sovereign will that any nation or people are elevated over another. ". . . And he (Nebuchadnezzar) shall stretch it out upon the land of Egypt", thereby breaking the power that Egypt had been allowed to reign supreme in for thousands of years. As Egypt is destined to decline, Babylon is simultaneously being elevated to become greater and more superior. "For promotion cometh neither from the east, nor from the west, nor from the south. But God is the judge: he putteth down one, and *setteth up another.*"

> "And I will scatter the Egyptians among the nations, and disperse them among the countries; and they shall know that I am the lord."—Ezekiel 30:26

The prophecy to 'scatter the Egyptians' is reiterated. Now they shall be mingled with other nations and shall be made to know that God is righteous. Lerone Bennett sets forth in his book: "For the human beings involved, the slave trade was a stupendous roulette wheel. The boats fanned out from Africa and scattered human freight over the Western Hemisphere. Around and around the wheel went, stopping here and there, sealing, wherever it stopped, the fate of mothers and fathers and their children to the nth generation.

It made a great deal of difference to the slaves where the dice of fate fell—whether they landed, for example, in a country where *the* word was the spanish *yo* or the french *je* or the English *I* . . ."

> "And it came to pass in the eleventh year, in the third month, in the first day of the month, that the word of the Lord came to me saying, Son of man, speak unto Pharaoh king of Egypt, and to his multitude: Whom art thou like in thy greatness?"—Ezekiel 31:1–2

110

This portion of prophecy came forth from God about four months later and the prophet is commanded to speak to Pharaoh *and to his multitude* (the people, princes, armies). He is instructed to pose this question to them: "Whom art thou like in thy greatness?", or 'Who is likened unto you? What other nation can compare to your greatness?' Egypt's greatness, based on skilled accomplishments, had made the nation widely known and honored, making it the leading continent in the ancient world with the oldest culture on earth. The nation had a uniqueness all its own that no other nation in the world could equal. The golden age of Ancient Egypt began during the rule of Zoser, also known as the first Memphite dynasty because Memphis was the seat of the royal government. Zoser encouraged the development of the arts and sciences. It was during this period that his counselor, Imhotep, a profound philosopher, distinguished for his great wisdom and sound judgement, probably designed the Step Pyramid, the first great structure of stone in history. These great works were equaled nowhere else in the ancient world.

On the subject of the pyramids, we borrowed a few enlightening comments from Paul Johnson's book, *The Civilization of Ancient Egypt*: "Pyramids are more complicated than they look. The Step Pyramid Imhotep built for Djoser (Zoser) is surprisingly sophisticated in design. It suggests some understanding of the concepts underlying the laws of stability. Imhotep was already building on a colossal scale: his Step Pyramid is 411 by 358 feet at base. Surprise is often expressed at the fact that the major pyramids combine huge size with very high standards of workmanship. The answer is that the greater the size, the higher the quality of workmanship demanded. The blocks had to be beautifully squared to ensure that they touched evenly, distributed the weight equally and prevented crumbling; accurate stone-dressing was also required to ensure that the internal weight-forces were properly distributed. Otherwise the pyramid might explode outwards and enormous quantities of stone crash down the sides. To combat the outward acting lateral forces produced by the sheer bulk and weight of the building, Imhotep had to invent inward-inclining buttress walls, which provided compensating inward-acting lateral forces. These walls, invisible from the outside, are an essential feature in ensuring the stability of big pyramids." *'Whom art thou like in thy greatness?'*

In his *Natural History*, Pliny the Elder condemned pyramids as 'an idle and foolish exhibition of royal wealth', but even he could not resist wondering 'how the stones were raised to so great a height'.

The Sphinx of Gizeh, one of the most famous statues in the world.
It has the body of a lion and a human head.

The Old Kingdom, which lasted for 500 years around the middle of the third millenium B.C., did not encompass all the accomplishments of Ancient Egyptian civilization. But in all essentials it was the matrix of the entire culture. In statescraft, religion, science, architecture, sculpture, low-relief and painting, in writing and thinking, the innovation of the Old Kingdom developed characteristic ideas and patterns which were later modified over 2,000 years, but never fundamentally changed." *'Whom art thou like in thy greatness?"*

> "Behold the Assyrian was a cedar in Lebanon with fair branches, and with a shadowing shroud, and of an high stature and his top was among the thick boughs. The water made him great, the deep set him up on high with her rivers running round about his plants, and sent out her little rivers unto all the trees of the field. Therefore his height was exalted above all the trees of the field, and his boughs were multiplied, and his branches became long because of the multitude of waters, when he shot forth. All the fowls of heaven made their nests in his boughs, and under his branches did all the beasts of the field bring forth their young, and under his shadow dwelt all great nations. Thus was he fair in his greatness, in the length of his branches: for his root was by great waters.—Ezekiel 31:3-7

Once again the demise of Egypt's greatness and prosperity is threatened. Using the downfall of the great nation of Assyria as an example, the prophet makes his appeal more imperative and more urgent than ever before. Ezekiel is commanded to appeal to Pharaoh's overweening pride and to liken his greatness and power to the Assyrians, whose vast empire had recently fallen at the hands of Nebuchadnezzar. "Show him," said the Lord, "how great a monarch the king of Assyria had been, a ruler who also had power and influence", implying to Pharaoh that if he ended up the same way, he would have so much more to lose than the Assyrians. The prophet was urged to impress upon Pharaoh that although the Assyrian nation was 'like a tall cedar in Lebanon'— had great abilities and importance and ranked high among the other great nations, as did Egypt—yet they were defeated at the hands of Nebuchadnezzar.

Beginning with verse four, Ezekiel began to relate to Pharaoh that from the beginning of civilization in Egypt, it was the Nile River that was the life blood of Egypt, "the waters made him great, the deep set him up on high". Egypt was fortunate to be further advanced in its society, culture, way of life and skills and abilities than the other nations, making it possible for the Egyptians to scale to heights that the other nations that came after had not yet reached. *'therefore his height was exalted above all the trees of the field'*. As a result of this advantage, history relates that Egypt began to increase and grow rapidly: "*. . . and his boughs were multiplied, and his branches became long because of the multitude of waters . . .*" Egyptian culture advanced and matured rapidly during the first two dynasties as Egypt began to overshadow other nations: "*and under his shadow dwelt all great nations . . .*" All because of an advantageous location, "*. . . for his root was by great waters.*" *Root* meaning 'his beginnings' was by great waters (the Nile River).

114

"The cedars in the garden of God could not hide him: the fir trees were not like his boughs, and the chestnut trees were not like his branches; *nor any tree in the garden of God was like unto him in his beauty.* I have made him fair by the multitude of his branches: so that all the trees of Eden, that were in the garden of God, envied him.—Ezekiel 31:8

Archaeological discoveries have overwhelmingly indicated that Africa was the cradle of mankind and that civilization started in Africa. In the beginning black people were in the forefront of civilization founding empires and dynasties and making important contributions which have contributed much to the progress that exists today.

In this portion of prophecy God commands Ezekiel to remind Pharaoh that the Egyptians stood out from all the other nations not only in power and prestige but also in hereditary physical beauty. In other words, God was cautioning Pharaoh and Egypt that failure to heed His warnings could result in their losing yet another important possession, an asset that the Egyptians were also famous for: their outstandingly handsome features. From her book, *A Tropical Dependency*, Flora Louisa Lugard quotes: "The Mosaic records allude to them (Ethiopians) frequently; but while they are described as the most powerful, the most just, *and the most beautiful of the human race*, they are constantly spoken of as black, and there seems to be no other conclusion to be drawn, than that at that remote period of history the leading race of the western world was a black race." (Quoted from *Before the Mayflower, A History of Black America*) Herodotus, the Greek historian, visited the country (Egypt) some five hundred years before Bethlehem. The Egyptians, he said, were "black and curly-haired". After visiting Egypt in 450 B.C. Herodotus also reported: "The furthest inhabited country towards the southwest is Ethiopia . . . The men *are the tallest in the world, the best-looking and the longest lived."* (Boston: Little, Brown. 1970, p. 29) 'The cedars . . . the fir trees . . .

115

Musicians in the Tomb of Nebamun, Thebes, from a wall-painting.

the chesnut trees . . . nor any tree in the garden of God was like unto him in his beauty.' The beauty of the Egyptians was such that, of all the other nations, there was no comparison for Egyptian beauty was extolled and admired because it excelled them all and outshone them all. The 'cedar trees, fir trees and chesnut trees' are symbolic of the other nations that 'could not hide him' or could not overshadow him'. There were many nationalities of beauty but none could compare to Egyptian beauty for Egypt overtopped them all. Another fascinating fact revealed in this prophecy is this statement: ". . . the fir trees were not like his boughs, and the chesnut trees were not like his

116

Mycerinus, Fourth Dynasty, is seen striding forward, in the characteristic posture of Egyptian dynastic art. His chief Queen was Chephren's eldest daughter.

branches . . ." In literal terms, the word *bough* and *branch* are similar but do not mean exactly the same thing. According to *Webster's Third New International Dictionary*, the word *bough*, derived from the Greek 'pechys' meaning forearm, is a prominent

outgrowth stemming from the main axis (as of a tree). A branch or branches are the several divisions stemming from the *bough*; therfore, the *bough* would be the first generation stemming from the first ancestor (main tree) and the *branches* would be the several divisions of the *bough*. Meaning that regardless of the presence in their ancestry of other ethnic strains, there would be no mistaking the presence of Egyptian blood because the famous Egyptian beauty would always emerge. This strong hereditary trait found among the Egyptians obviously was not found commonly among the other nations: ". . . the fir trees were not like his boughs, and the chesnut trees were not like his branches." The historian Herodotus referred to it as ". . . a character always retained despite alien influence brought to bear on them from time to time." The least amount of Egyptian blood in the heritage carried the genes for this fabulous physical beauty. 'I have made him fair . . .' In the

118

words of Matthew Henry: "He was comely with the comeliness that God had placed upon him, so as to be very beautiful to the eye." In spite of all the other beauty that existed at that time, God chose to glorify and exalt Egyptian beauty above all the rest. "I have made him fair by the multitude of his branches, meaning that the average Egyptian offspring was a typical beauty.

All the grace of adolescence.

". . . So that all the trees of Eden, that were in the garden of God, *envied him*." So well-known was the distinguished beauty of the Egyptians that it was the envy of the ancient world. Egyptian good looks were universally known, admired and envied. The other "trees" were shrubs by comparison. The fact that such exquisite beauty was passed down intact from generation to generation obviously was entirely God's doing. It was His to give; it was

119

also His to take, which is precisely what God is threatening to do. The glory of handsome good looks enjoyed by the Egyptians for thousands of years was about to be diminished. In this appeal to the ego, the prophet warns that the Egyptians would one day no longer stand out from all other nations for their handsome looks. Just as they carried strong hereditary genes for beauty, they would one day carry genes for very unappealing looks.

Concerning "all the trees of Eden, that were in the garden of God", the prophet is in reference to the Egyptians' ancestral beginnings that originated in the *garden of Eden*. From history it is recorded that the Ethiopians considered themselves to be of greater antiquity than any other nation. It is very likely that the Ancient Egyptians were aware of the fact that they were descended from the first man, Adam. Moreover, the other nations of the Ancient World were probably aware of this fact as well. Using the research of competent Biblical scholars and scientists, Walter Arthur McCray states it quite well: "The outdated view teaches that humanity's origin is found, not in Egypt Africa, but in Asia, in lower Mesopotamia in the area of the Tigris-Euphrates Valley. Though the verses in Genesis 2:8–14 explaining the geography of the Garden of Eden do appear to reference the Mesopotamian areas, it must be kept in mind that the names of the river head-streams Pishon, Gihon, Tigris, and Euphrates were names given to rivers thousands, if not millions, of years following God's creation of humanity and placing them in the Garden of Eden.

Nevertheless, whether one accepts the latter view, that humanity began in Asia, or the more substantiated view, that humanity began in Egypt, Africa, *there is a single thread that is common to both. Humanity, at its outset was indeed black*, a fact that is affirmed by the first civilizations which emerged. For Asia's lower Mesopotamian civilizations were black (Rashidi, JAC, p. 163; quoting Diop, in *Great African Thinkers*, p.235). The Sumerians were the "founders and guardians of West Asia's oldest known civilization" (Rashidi, JAC, p.163).

120

It is a noted fact that *wherever* ancient civilizations have emerged on the face of the earth, they were black. Whether in Egypt, Ethiopia, Sumer, Asia, North America or South America, each cultural center of the ancient world was "Hamitic in origin". Blacks are the progenitors of humanity and the creative originators of culture and civilizations."

Interestingly, the January 1988 *Newsweek Magazine* published a scientific discovery which may in fact be a confirmation that the original man and woman, Adam and Eve, were indeed black. Genetic researchers were able to persuade 147 pregnant women in America with ancestors from Africa, Europe, the Middle East and Asia, to donate their babies placentas to science. The final report read something like this: "The babies' DNA seemed to form a family tree *rooted* in Africa. The DNA fell into two general categories, one found only in some babies of recent African descent, and a second found in everyone else *and the other Africans.* There was more diversity among the exclusively African group's DNA, suggesting that it had accumulated more mutations because *it had been around longer*—and thus was the longest branch of the family tree. Apparently, the DNA tree began in Africa, and then at some point a group of Africans emigrated, splitting off to form a second branch of DNA and carrying it to the rest of the world.

In the meantime, there is one temporary candidate for an Adam—not the one scientists are looking for but one defined simply as a man from whom we are all descended. Since we are all descended from Eve's daughters, any common male ancestor of theirs would be a common ancestor to everyone today. This wouldn't necessarily be Eve's husband. For all we know, she may have had more than one. But her daughters all certainly had the same maternal grandfather. So, at least for now, *the only safe conclusion is that Adam was Eve's Father.*" What a triumph for the word of God! for this is precisely what the Bible teaches. "And the rib, which the Lord God had taken from man, made he a woman, and brought her unto the man. And Adam said, This is now bone of my bones, and flesh of my flesh: she shall be called Woman, because she was taken out of man." (Genesis 2:22–23). Adam was not only Eve's husband, he was also her father.

From the very beginning of Bible history, the Bible is basically ethnogeographic, concerned primarily with the origin and classification of the nations of the ancient world: their families, the languages they spoke, the lands in which they lived, and the nations to which they belonged. During Bible times, blackness was not regarded with shame and public reproach because God had glorified blackness and made it a thing of beauty. To be black was a type of glorification, a badge of honor that was respected among the nations and throughout the ancient world because of the antiquity that accompanied it, signifying a longer hereditary line than other races. Lerone Bennett Jr. sums it up: "Looking back on that age from our own, one is struck by what seems to be an absence of color consciousness. Back there, in the beginning, blackness did not seem to be an occasion for obloquy. In fact, the reverse seems to have been true, for whites were sometimes ridiculed for the unnatural whiteness of their skin.

During this critical period in the evolution of man, Blacks were known and honored throughout the ancient world. One of the clearest examples of this is the great mural of a procession from a tomb of Thebes in the time of Thotmes III. The Egyptians and Ethiopians in the procession are painted in the usual brown and black colors, but thirty-seven whites in the procession are rendered in white tones. Who are they? G. A. Hoskins said they were probably 'white slaves of the king of Ethiopia sent to the Egyptian king as the most acceptable present.'

Walter Arthur McCray also states: ". . . therefore the existence of whiteness and the development of "white" people occured later in the history of humanity. In other words, the evidence—Biblical evidence, archaeological evidence, and DNA-wise evidence— points in the direction that blackness is humanity's norm and whiteness is the exception rather than the rule, the derivation, not the origination." (*The Black Presence in the Bible*).

In order to diminish the importance of black skin and the dignity and pride that went with it, God chose to exalt the white man whose skin color was in direct contrast by comparison to the black man's skin. The prophet warns Pharaoh and Egypt that not only would there be a diminishing of their good looks but the blackness that enhanced their beautiful features and was also a badge of honor recognized among nations, would one day be more of a curse to them than a blessing! 'The cedars . . . the fir trees . . . the chesnut trees . . . *nor any tree in the garden of God was like unto him in his beauty*' It is today an obvious fact that God not only elevated the white man and glorified whiteness of the skin, but He also magnified it with the very same grandeur, glory and nobility that was once the proud possession of the black race. The descension of the Egyptians as a race and as a nation was clearly ordained of God because of their wickedness and disobedience to Him. No nation, no matter how great and powerful, can afford to boldly ignore the commandments of God and expect to continue to prosper in the midst of their sin and disobedience.

> "Therefore thus saith the Lord God; Because thou hast lifted up thyself in height, and he hath shot up his top among the thick boughs, and his heart is lifted up in his height; I have therefore delivered him into the hand of the mighty one of the heathen; he shall surely deal with him: I have driven him out for his wickedness."—Ezekiel 31:10-11

To say that Pharaoh and the Egyptians had practically everything any nation could desire would certainly be putting it mildly. According to Matthew Henry: ". . . he (Pharaoh) had abundance of wealth to support his power and grandeur; he had vast treasures, large stores and magazines (storehouses, armorys), constant revenues coming in by taxes, customs and crown rents; these enabled him to strengthen and secure his interests everywhere . . . It is rare to find an humble spirit in the midst of great accomplishments." 'Because thou hast lifted up thyself in height, and hath shot up his top among the thick boughs, and *his heart is lifted up in his height.*' Clearly, the pride of the Egyptians also helped to destroy Egypt. 'I have therefore delivered him into the hand of the mighty one of the heathen; he shall surely deal with him: I have driven him out for his wickedness.' Again Matthew Henry declares: ". . . God is the judge . . . and when He pleases He can extirpate and expel those who think themselves, and seem to others, to have taken deepest root. *And the mightiest ones of the heathens could not gain their point against those they contended with if the Almighty did not Himself deliver them into their hands.* It is his own sin that procures his ruin."

> "And *strangers, the terrible of the nations,* have cut him off, and have left him: upon the mountains and in all the valleys his branches are fallen, and his boughs are broken by all the rivers of the land; and all the people of the earth are gone down from his shadow, and have left him. Upon his ruin shall all the fowls of the heaven remain, and all the beasts of the field shall be upon his branches: To the end that none of all the trees by the waters exalt themselves for their height, neither shoot up their top among the thick boughs, neither their trees stand up in their height, all that drink water: *for they are all delivered unto death, to the nether parts of the earth, in the midst of the children of men, with them that go down to the pit.*"—Ezekiel 31:12–14

God spoke this prophecy as if it were already a foregone conclusion indeed—so sure is He of what He must allow to be. This prediction foretells the total takeover of the continent by "strangers, the terrible (mighty) of the nations . . .", who will cut him off and leave him. Looking back upon the state of Africa for the past 300 years, it is clear to see that it is the outsiders (strangers), the mighty of the nations who have been responsible for the vast exploitation of the continent, "having seized", says Matthew Henry, "upon parts of his dominion and forced them out of his hands . . ."

". . . His branches are fallen, and his boughs are broken by all the rivers of the land . . ." His powerful princes, from the youngest (his branches) to the eldest (his boughs) are overcome (fallen) and their powers broken . . . and all the people of the earth are gone down from his shadow, and have left him . . ." All those who once enjoyed basking in the mighty shadow (protection) of Egypt shall seek to her no more for her protection. No country would concern itself anymore with the affairs of Egypt. The Egyptians would be deserted and totally abandoned by other nations; left to the mercy of strangers who would do nothing to alleviate or change the situation.

". . . Upon his ruin shall all the fowls of the heaven remain, and all the beasts of the field shall be upon his branches . . ." The scavengers shall all take advantage of his ruin and downfall, from one end of the continent to the other, upon the mountains and in all the valleys. This statement from the 1983 *Encyclopaedia Britannica* reads: "In 1920 every square mile of the African continent except the independent states of Ethiopia and Liberia was under colonial rule or protection or was claimed by one or the other of the European colonial powers. By the early 1950s however, African nationalism and the rise of independence movements were widespread, a development that marked the beginning of the rapid decline of imperial power in Africa."

Liberia has never been under colonial rule. Only for a brief period was Ethiopia under foreign rule. Dictator Mussolini and his troops invaded Ethiopia in 1935. The Ethiopian emperor pleaded in vain before the League of Nations for military aid, which was denied, and Ethiopia was therefore defeated in 1936. In 1941 British and Commonwealth forces drove the Italians out.

The day of the total demise of Egypt, as a nation and as a people, would surely come. The Egyptians shall never rise up again and be exalted. ". . . To the end that none of all the trees by the waters exalt themselves for their height, neither shoot up their top among the thick boughs, neither their trees stand up in their height . . ." In that day they shall find themselves powerless and of no consequence; past glories shall mean nothing. '. . . neither their trees stand up in their height . . .' no more shall they stand out and excel above all the other nations for their exceptional abilities. ". . . all that drink water . . .", from the youngest to the eldest. For they are all delivered to their several destinies: *death* (some were slated to die presently), *to the nether parts of the earth* (some to be scattered among the nations and dispersed among the countries) *in the midst of the children of men* (some were destined to remain on the continent to suffer at the hands of heathens).

> "Thus saith the Lord God, In the day when he went down to the grave I caused a mourning: I covered the deep for him, and I restrained the floods thereof, and the great waters were stayed: and I caused Lebanon to mourn for him, and all the trees of the field fainted for him. I made the nations to shake at the sound of his fall, when I cast him down to hell with them that descend into the pit: and all the trees of Eden, the choice and best of Lebanon, all that drink water, shall be comforted in the nether parts of the earth. They also went down into hell with him unto them that be slain with the sword; and they that were his arm, that dwelt under his shadow in the midst of the heathen."—Ezekiel 31:15-17

The gravity of Egypt's pending downfall is marked by the word 'grave' which describes the depth of Egypt's descension, commencing the beginning of the end of the reign of Egypt as a great and prosperous nation, one that ruled over other nations. ". . . I caused a mourning . . ." for this day would also mark the beginning of a future that no other nation has had to endure, one filled with all the dehumanizing and degrading horrors of slavery, exploitation, hopelessness and despair, the like of which has yet to be equaled.

". . . I covered the deep for him, and I restrained the floods thereof, and the great waters were stayed . . ." Business and foreign trade (transacted mainly by means of ships) 'were stayed' (temporarily halted) in recognition of the loss of this monarch and his monarchy. ". . . and I caused *Lebanon* to mourn for him, and all the trees of the field fainted for him . . .", meaning 'I caused all the business world, that knew him well, to mourn the loss of his participation, especially Lebanon.' The country of Lebanon, was settled around 2,000 B.C. by some people the Greeks called Phoenicians, which means "dark-skinned", who began to settle along the strip of land between the mountains of Lebanon and the sea. The Phoenicians were mariners and seafarers, who made their living trading along caravan routes and shipping lanes. "But above all, says the *New Bible Dictionary*, "Lebanon's cedars and conifers (firs, cypresses) furnished the finest building timber in the ancient East, *sought by the rulers of Egypt*, Mesopotamia and Syria-Palestine alike. The most celebrated of such deliveries of timber were those sent to Solomon by Hiram I of Tyre for the temple at Jerusalem. The firs of Lebanon . . . provided ships for Tyre and sacred barges for Egypt as well as furniture. Wood for the second Jerusalem temple was also cut in Lebanon.

The Lebanon timber-trade goes back to the earliest times. The 4th Dynasty Pharaoh Snofru fetched 40 shiploads of cedars as early as 2600 B.C., and various of his successors followed suit in later centuries. Byblos in particular became virtually an Egyptian dependency and its princes thoroughly assimilated to Egyptian culture, even writing their Semitic names in hieroglyphs. In exchange for timber, they received handsome gold jewelry from the 12th Dynasty Pharaoh (1900–1800 B.C.).

When the New Kingdom Pharaohs conquered Syria they exacted a regular annual tribute of 'genuine cedar of Lebanon'; and a relief of Sethos I actually depicts the Syrian princes hewing down the timbers of Lebanon for the Pharaoh. In later days (20th Dynasty) the Pharaohs had to pay handsomely for such timber. The fertility and fruitfulness of the Lebanon region are often referred to in Scripture, for the mighty cedars were apt symbols of earthly pride as well as symbols of majesty and strength. ". . . and I caused Lebanon to mourn for him . . ." In view of the many centuries of

127

business transactions between Egypt and Lebanon, understandably they, along with the other nations, would surely mourn the loss of one of its oldest and wealthiest patrons. ". . . and all the trees of the field fainted for him . . ." or, They all nearly passed out when they heard of it. A general lamentation was heard universally as nations began to mourn the demise of such a powerful one. ". . . I made the nations to shake at the sound of his fall . . ." The downfall of this mighty monarch and his great nation caused the other nations to tremble (shake) at the news and to be struck with astonishment that so mighty a prince could be brought so low. It was a shock to all their confidences for, after all, this was not just any nation, but the great and mighty Egypt. ". . . And all the trees of Eden, the choice and best of Lebanon, all that drink water shall be comforted in the nether parts of the earth." Even they that dwell in the farthest (nether) parts of the world shall be visibly disturbed and shaken at the news of Egypt's fall, yet for envy, shall they be comforted that this mighty nation has been brought down from her lofty perch. Yet, they themselves shall fare no better for "they also went down into hell with him unto them that be slain with the sword . . ." Even "they that were his arm (strong help), that dwelt under his shadow in the midst of the heathens."

> "To whom art thou thus like in glory and in greatness among the trees of Eden? Yet shalt thou be brought down with the trees of Eden unto the nether parts of the earth: thou shalt lie in the midst of the uncircumcised with them that be slain by the sword. This is Pharaoh and all his multitude, saith the Lord God."—Ezekiel 31:18

In conclusion of this portion of prophecy, the prophet attempts once more to appeal to Pharaoh's conceited sense of pride and importance, "To whom art thou thus like in glory and in greatness among the trees of Eden (the other nations)?" No other nation can compare in glory and greatness for Egypt is the most influential nation in the world. "Yet shalt thou be brought down with the trees of Eden unto the nether parts of the earth . . ." The Assyrian empire, after having reigned in Asia for four centuries, had been overthrown by Nebuchadnezzar. The prophet forewarns that in spite of Egypt's greatness, it shall be brought down to the very level of the other great nations.

Over ninety percent of Bible commentaries and expositories have stated that this thirty-first chapter of Ezekiel is in reference to the Assyrians, but that there be no mistake as to whom the Lord is in reference to, the Prophet declares: *"This is Pharaoh and all his multitude, saith the Lord God."*

Ezekiel Chapter 32

"And Huetius gives this reason why none but God can foretell things to come, because *every effect* depends upon an infinite number of *preceding causes*, all which, in their order, must be known to him that foretells the effect, and therefore to God only, for He alone is omniscient.

Still we are upon the destruction of Pharaoh and Egypt, which is wonderfully enlarged upon, and with a great deal of emphasis. When we read so very much of Egypt's ruin, no less than six several prophecies at divers times delivered concerning it, we are ready to think, *surely there is some special reason for it.*" (Copied from the preface of *Matthew Henry's commentary Vol. IV*, written by his hand July 18, 1712).

> "And it came to pass in the twelfth month, in the first day of the month, that the word of the Lord came unto me saying, Son of man, take up a lamentation for Pharaoh king of Egypt, and say unto him, Thou art like a young lion of the nations, and thou art as a whale in the seas: and thou camest forth with thy rivers, and troubledst the waters with thy feet, and foulest their rivers."— Ezekiel 32:1–2

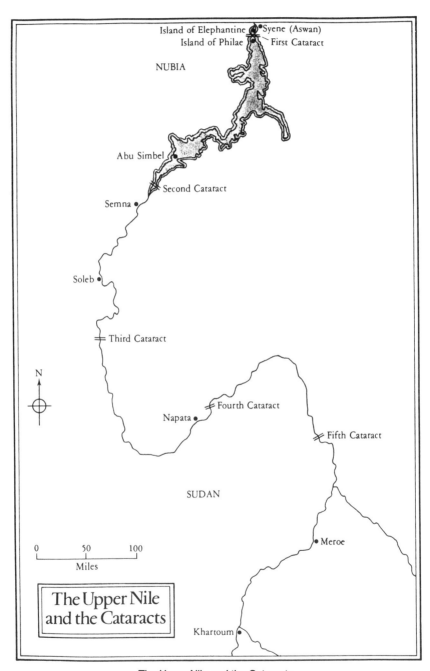

The Upper Nile and the Cataracts

The prophet is commanded once again to appeal to Pharaoh through his vain and conceited pride, by likening his power and greatness to that of the lion: its majesty and strength, royalty and courage. ". . . Thou art like a young lion of the nations . . ." And as a whale in the seas which dominates the waters. Ezekiel reminds him that his beginnings are as ancient as the Nile River, itself: ". . . and thou camest forth with thy rivers . . ." To mention the Nile River was the same as mentioning the land of Egypt for, in the eyes of the world, they were practically one and the same. For centuries there was a mystery surrounding the Nile River. How could there be such a big river in such a dry land? It took a whole series of explorations from about 1615 to about 1900 to trace the complete length of the Nile. Finally it was discovered that branches of this important river have their sources in three lakes: Lake Victoria, Lake Tana, and Lake Albert, all in the hot wet heartland of Africa. The *New Bible Dictionary* quotes: "The most remarkable feature of the Nile is its yearly rise and flooding over its banks, without which Egypt would be as desolate as the deserts on the east and west of it." Wherever the Nile waters reach, vegetation can grow, life can exist. Egypt's agriculture depended wholly upon the Nile. A high flood produced the splendid crops that made Egypt's agricultural wealth proverbial. The Nile, in dominating Egypt's agriculture, not only supported crops but formed also the marshes for pasture and papyrus and contained a wealth of fish caught by both line and net. The Nile was also Egypt's main arterial highway; boats could sail north by merely going with the stream, and could as readily sail south with the aid of the cool north wind from the Meditteranean." However, the prophet declares, the power and wealth afforded by the river was not used rightly by the Egyptians.

". . . And thou . . . trouble the waters with thy feet, and foulest their rivers." The Nile itself was one of the many gods the Egyptians worshipped. In their religious beliefs, the spirit of the Nile-flood was the god Ha'pi, bringer of fertility and abundance.

"Thus saith the Lord God; *I will therefore spread out my net over thee with a company of many people*; and they shall bring thee up in my net."—Ezekiel 32:3

The Arabic root word for net is 'kmr' which means overcome or cover. In the Hebrew it is 'mikmoret' which referred to the dragnet the Egyptian fishermen used to spread over the waters. The truer meaning here is *network*, referring to a company of many people, or nations. Is there any wonder that there are so many nations that have dominated the continent of Africa for the past 300 years? 'My Net' is a definite depiction of ownership, meaning God Himself chose each one of the nations that served as a net or snare for Africa. From that time on, the history of Africa has been, with the exception of Ethiopia and Liberia, a story of the exploration, conquest and colonization of the continent by various nations of Europe and Asia. Rules for the acquiring of African lands were laid down at the conference in Berlin in 1884–1885. In 1908 the Congo Free State was handed over to Belgium. Its name was changed to the Belgian Congo. France, however, had more territory in Africa than any other nation but Great Britain's holdings were far more valuable. In the Boer War, (1899–1902) Britain won the Transvaal and the Orange Free State from the Dutch settlers, the Boers. These states, rich in diamonds and gold, became part of the Union of South Africa.

The various nations defined their boundaries and laid down rules for future occupation on the coasts of Africa and for navigation of the Congo and Niger Rivers. Most important was the rule that when a power acquired new territory in Africa, it must notify the other powers. In 1915 the various nations with territories in Africa were as follows:

France.....................4,403,401 square miles
Great Britain...........3,514,271 square miles
Belgium ....909,654 square miles
Germany ....931,460 square miles

Portugal .... 793,980 square miles
Italy .... 591,230 square miles
Spain .... 84,814 square miles

"... I will therefore spread out my net over thee *with a company of many people*: and they shall bring thee up in my net," meaning they shall force him out of his heritage and dislodge him out of his possessions. Obviously Pharaoh had the mistaken notion that Egypt was invincible, incapable of being conquered, beaten or defeated.

> "Then will I leave thee upon the land, I will cast thee forth upon the open field, and will cause all the fowls of the heaven to remain upon thee and I will fill the beasts of the whole earth with thee."—Ezekiel 32:4

No more shall the Egyptians be known to navigate the waters as before: "Then will I leave thee upon the land ..." Because of the much trading with other nations, the Egyptians were familiar with water travel and in 332 B.C. invented the sail for sailboats. Furthermore, their abode shall no longer be associated with the great Nile River, "... I will cast thee forth upon the open fields ...", or meaning 'I will throw you out and scatter you in every direction (upon the open fields)'. There are yet tribes in Africa that have never been exposed to civilization as we know it.

"... And I will fill the beasts of the whole earth with thee." In Africa, sub-Sahara is the natural habitat of a variety of many wild animals, including the buffalo, rhinoceros, zebra, gnu, antelope, giraffe, lion, panther, and the so-called African tiger which is really a leopard. The hyena, ape and monkey live in the forests south of the equator. In the densest forests live the great apes, baboons, gorillas and chimpanzees. Elephants formerly roamed freely all over the continent but they have been so much hunted for their ivory tusks that they are no longer common. The ostrich is found on the southern savannahs. In the swamps and rivers are the

crocodile, hippo, snake, fox, jackal, okapi, quagga, pygmy
Mauritanian ass, the huge python, warthog, deer, mongoose and
numerous others. ". . . I will fill the beasts of the whole earth with
thee."

"And I will lay thy flesh upon the mountains, and fill the valleys
with thy height. I will also water with thy blood the land wherein
thou swimmest, even to the mountains; and the rivers shall be full
of thee."—Ezekiel 32:5–6

"The fall of Pharaoh represents the fall of the world-power
before the sovereignty of God." (*Bible Commentary on the Old
Testament* 1980). This prophecy sets forth the deep impression
which the fall of Egypt shall make upon neighboring nations to
see such greatness come to nothing, and that all the gods of Egypt
were not able to deliver them. In the day of the Lord when God
shall judge Egypt, ". . . I will lay thy flesh upon the mountains,
and fill the valleys with thy height." In other words, these judgements of God shall not be hidden from the eyes of the world. The
news of their destruction shall reach from the highest mountain to
the lowest valley, matching the height to which they were once
elevated; the same degree to which they were put up, shall be the

same degree to which they shall be put down. "I will also water with thy blood the land . . . even to the mountains . . ." Such vast quantities of blood shall be shed in such abundance that it shall seem to flow like water, even to the mountains.

> "And when I shall put thee out, I will cover the heaven, and make the stars thereof dark; I will cover the sun with a cloud, and the moon shall not give her light. All the bright lights of heaven will I make dark over thee, *and set darkness upon thy land, saith the Lord God.*"—Ezekiel 32:7–8

". . . And when I shall *put thee out* . . ." (R.V. extinguish thee). Or when I shall put out your bright lights that you shall no longer shine or stand out in the midst of the nations. Keep in mind that it is God who glorifies a nation and makes it to stand out in the midst of other nations. The Egyptians' creative imagination and abilities to originate designs and inventions never before revealed to mankind, in addition to the great wisdom they were noted for, were *all* inspired by Almighty God Himself. "I will cover the heaven, and make the stars thereof dark . . ." The Lord literally "opened the heavens" exceedingly for the Egyptians, in a way that He did not do for other nations, imparting to them knowledge and abilities that modern scientists even today have not figured out. One of the greatest Egyptian contributions to world knowledge was astronomy. A major achievement of the Egyptian astronomers was the establishment of a solar calendar, based on a year of 365 days and consisting of twelve 30-day months. By observing the stars, the Egyptians knew the approximate length of a year. They dated their first day from the rising of the star Sirius in mid-July, which corresponded with the beginning of the annual Nile River flood. However, the Lord has declared, ". . . when I shall put thee out . . ."(extinguish your smarts and abilities) they shall no more have the ability to interpret the great wonders of astronomy, ". . . I will cover the heaven, and make the stars thereof dark . . ."

"I will cover the sun with a cloud, and the moon shall not give her light." Bumper crops that the Egyptians always had in abundance were possible, not only because of the Nile River, but also because of their knowledge of the stars and phases of the moon, thereby making it possible for them to plant at the right time as well as harvest. The Egyptians understood the significance of the role that the stars, moon and the heavenlies played in certain functions of nature that take place here on the earth. God, who ordained the purpose of the heavenlies from the beginning of time, had endowed the Egyptians with an outstanding knowledge of the heavenlies (the stars, moon, sun) and how they effected certain natural functions in the earth. It is a skill and a know-how that has almost vanished because of the misuse and abuse of astrology and the zodiac signs that has come about in recent years in the form of horoscopes and stargazing and as a result, many Christians have shied away from acknowledging the importance of the heavenly bodies. However, one must keep in mind the real purpose of the heavenlies: "And God said, Let there be lights (stars, moon, sun) in the firmament of the heaven to divide the day from the night: *and let them be for signs, and for seasons, and for days, and years.*" (Genesis 1:14). "He *appointed the moon for seasons* . . ." (Psalms 104:19). Through their study of astronomy, the Egyptians were able to employ their knowledge of signs and seasons to determine certain days and the length of a year, and especially to apply it to their seedtime and harvest time. The practice yet exists among many modern-day farmers who seldom will begin to set out seed for planting without first consulting their *Farmers' Almanac*, a planting guide book that illustrates the phases and positions of the moon. "I will cover the sun with a cloud, and the moon shall not give her light . . ." They shall no more excel in the knowledge and wisdom of the heavenlies.

"All the bright lights of heaven will I make dark over thee . . ." When God totally shuts up heaven over a nation, any nation, because of sin, it is then that divinely inspired knowledge and inspirations shall be no more. No new inventions, ideas, creations, enlightenments, visions and inventive dreams are inspired to that nation. Innovative thoughts and creative imaginations for new devices and witty inventions are no longer imparted. "All the bright lights of heaven will I make dark over thee . . . and set darkness upon thy land, saith the Lord God." Darkness represents *ignorance*; total ignorance shall set in upon the land. For this reason Africa has often been referred to for centuries as the *Dark Continent* or *Darkest Africa*. The prophet Micah makes reference to this type of condition in chapter 3:6–7: "Therefore night shall be unto you, that ye shall not have a vision; and it shall be dark unto you, *that ye shall not divine*; and the sun shall go down over the prophets (leaders) and the day shall be dark over them. Then shall the seers be ashamed, and the diviners confounded: yea, they shall all cover their lips; for there is no answer of God."

God has determined to close the minds of the Egyptians that they shall never again, as a nation, impress the world with their great wisdom and knowledge. No new inspirations, such as has been in the past, will anymore originate from the land of Egypt. The Egyptians, famous for the invention of the sun dial and the water clock, are also believed to have been the first to make writing paper. They also had copper mines and used bronze. The knowledge of geometry was a necessity for measuring land because the landmarks were periodically obliterated by the annual floods of the Nile River and the accurate construction of the pyramids required a mastery of measurements in two and three dimensions. Egyptian mathematicians solved the area of the triangle and the circle. They also had excellent knowledge of physiology and bone surgery, and medical schools were attached to some of the temples. About 2600 B.C. they already excelled in spinning and weaving linen cloth, masonry, and making cosmetics. They had also invented leather rolls, pens and ink. There can be no doubt that they were the first to master the art of building in stone. In every field of knowledge known to the Ancients, the Egyptians had much to offer for they had initiated the use of them. The biggest mistake the Egyptians made was that they refused to acknowledge Jehovah God as the creator and giver of all good things. Instead, they used God-given abilities to glorify their many false gods. Herodotus, the Greek writer considered the Egyptians to be "religious to excess, far beyond any other race of men. Bulls, cows, cats, dogs, crocodiles, mongoose, shrew-mice, hawks, falcons, and other animals or birds were all sacred to some god or other . . ."

Paul Johnson states: "The Egyptian craftsman did not perform for the human eye but the divine. His splendid vases were transferred direct from workshop to tomb and buried in eternal darkness. Later, the great sculptures were usually walled up in stygian rooms to which human access was totally forbidden. These works were perfected to satisfy the gods and if they gave delight to human eyes it was coincidental . . . Thus right at the very beginning of their cultural efflorescence the Egyptians manifested an *unbending will* to devote their creative skills to their gods."

"I shall set darkness (ignorance) upon thy land . . ." The bush as well as the large Sahara Desert kept sub-Sahara Africa isolated from civilization for many centuries. It was a land of mystery and danger for no one knew what sort of people lived in the heart of the continent, therefore, for many centuries it was known as the Dark Continent. 'I shall set darkness (ignorance) upon thy land . . ." Africa's main problem today is to educate its people. Protestant and Roman Catholic missionaries have, through the years, attempted the task but many tribal chiefs and government officials have preferred to keep the people ignorant for fear they shall rebel against their primitive living conditions. The very high percentage of illiteracy in Africa makes it hard to believe that these are the descendants of the wisest, most intelligent people that ever graced the face of the earth: *the Ancient Egyptians.*

Isaiah had already prophesied that, ". . . the spirit of Egypt shall fail in the midst thereof . . ." (Isaiah 19:3). History relates that after the Persian conquest of Egypt, the spirit of the great

Egyptian culture began to fade, and by the time of the Roman conquest, Egyptian civilization was no longer the independent, creative force it once was. The irony of it all is that when expressions of praise are lauded upon "the first black to excell in this field" and "the first black to do outstandingly in that field"—it's hard to believe that we are simply on the way back up—again!

139

One of the many sphinxes in Egypt.

"I will vex the hearts of many people, when I shall bring thy destruction among the nations, into the countries which thou hast not known."—Ezekiel 32:9

Civil rights demonstration, Birmingham

The question that has most often come to the minds of many black people, ever since the first black slaves were shipped over from Africa is, "Why do most white people hate black people so intensely? Is it really because of their blackness?" Many have hazarded the guess that they secretly harbour a deep-down fear of black people, a fear that they themselves cannot explain. However, the real answer lies in the fact that God declared that He would 'vex the hearts of many people . . . among the nations (and) the countries . . ." The word *vex*, according to *Vine's*, means to disturb trouble to irritate. Roughly paraphrased, the verse would read: "I shall stir up or irritate their hearts against you when

141

you enter into their lands. Your presence shall stir up hatred and bitterness in the hearts of many of the people." In other words, God stirred up hatred in their hearts to serve His divine purpose in order to fulfill what He had prophesied against the Egyptians. It must be noted that God did not say *all* the people because He also stirred compassion in the hearts of many white people who sympathized with the plight of black people, helping to eventually bring about their freedom from slavery. 'I will vex (irritate) the hearts of many people, *when I shall bring thy destruction among the nations, into the countries which thou hast not known."* In other words, the curse of the prophecy will follow you no matter where you are or where you go. Your presence shall be received with hatred and dislike in countries you were never familiar with before. You shall not be welcomed with open arms.

The hearts of many people were indeed 'vexed' or stirred up against the black man, giving birth to such organizations as the Ku Klux Klan about the year 1866, after the War between the States. Riding at night, they draped themselves in white sheets, wearing masks and white cardboard hats, using disguises, secrecy and terror that were directed mainly against black people. Their activities also included burning fiery crosses on black people's properties, besides flogging, lynching and torturing them to keep them from their voting rights and other privileges granted to them in the Constitution. This group and many other types of hate groups sprang up because God had already declared that this kind of extreme dislike would emerge "when I shall bring thy destruction among the nations; into the countries which thou hast not known."

Racism, itself was also forged and newly instituted by the hand of God Himself, to bring to pass what He had already ordained to be. According to the *1983 Encyclopaedia Britannica:* "As a well-developed theory, racism is a fairly recent phenomenom, even in Western history. The 18th century was predominantly environmentalist in its outlook; the science of that day tended to attribute social behaviour either to climactic and geographical environment or to sociocultural factors. Racism as a widely accepted "scientific" theory of behaviour *did not appear until the 19th century*, which was the age of racism par excellence. In Africa, the initial contacts between Portuguese and Africans were relatively free of racism and relatively peaceful and friendly . . . There is, for example, a record of a friendly correspondence between the kings of Portugal and Kongo and of an exchange of ambassadors . . . Even when Europeans first came into more extensive direct contact with large numbers of dark-skinned peoples, as a result of their colonial expansion starting in the late 15th century, *Racism took some time to develop*." 'I will . . . vex the hearts of many people.'

A surprising fact comes from an excerpt from Lerone Bennett: ". . . white people did not seem to know that they were white. It appears from surviving evidence that the first white colonists had no concept of themselves as *white* people. The legal documents identified whites as Englishmen and/or Christians. The word *white*, with its burden of arrogance and biological pride, *developed late in the century, as a direct result of slavery and the organized debasement of Blacks* . . . The institution of slavery itself led to the categorization of "white" people and "black" people, with the concept that black people were backward and inferior." Even after the slave trade between Africa, Europe and the Americas was abolished in the 19th century, this concept continued to survive and is only now disappearing.

The Netherlands and Great Britain were responsible for the growth of the most racist colonial societies that the world has ever known—namely, South Africa, the United States, and Australia. The South African policy of apartheid has become a byword for racial discrimination and, next to the Nazi policy of genocide against Jews, represents the most extreme and systematic form of racism practiced in a modern society. "I will vex the hearts of many people."

143

The question that now comes to mind is, of all the other races and nationalities in the world that God could have chosen to rule over black people, *why did he choose the white race?* In view of the ancestral background of the black man, the old argument of superior intelligence just doesn't hold anymore. Was it because they were the ones most capable of such strong and lasting hatred that could endure over hundreds of years, from generation to generation, and still maintain its great intensity? Was this the quality that God, who knows all men's hearts, was seeking when He decided to select a 'cruel lord and a fierce king' to rule over blacks? After all, we must keep in mind that God intended that His punishment of black people should continue, with no let-up, through the centuries, until the prophecy was finally fulfilled.

> "Yea, I will make many people *amazed at thee*, and their kings shall be horribly afraid for thee, when I shall brandish my sword before them; and they shall tremble at every moment, every man for his own life, *in the day of thy fall*."—Ezekiel 32:10

"Amazed", meaning surprised, struck, stems from the root word *ekstasis*, a 'standing out', exceedingly struck in mind, as to be greatly astonished. ". . . and their kings shall be horribly afraid for thee . . ." Their amazement and astonishment "at thee" shall be because of the unpleasantness of the black man's appearance to Western European concepts of beauty—repugnant and uncomely. An appearance so alien and unlikeable as to arouse antagonism and aversion. ". . . I will make many people *amazed at thee* . . ." In Ezekiel chapter 31, the prophet reminded Pharaoh that it was God who had favored Egypt with outstanding beauty, ". . . not any tree in the garden of God was like unto him in his beauty." He was warned not to take this fact for granted, an unusual phenomenon not found commonly among the other nations: ". . . I have made him fair . . . so that all the trees of Eden, that were in the garden of God, envied him." The Egyptians chose to ignore

144

this warning also, therefore God gave them over to their own devices. allowing sin and the consequences of sin, continuing through the many centuries, to take its toll, so that when Africa was penetrated and invaded by Europeans, the great beauty that Egyptians had been noted for had all but completely vanished.

It is a recorded and historical fact that when African natives were first shipped to other countries, upon their arrival they were

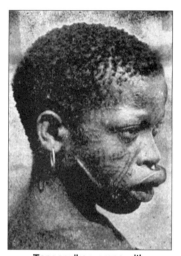

Tanganyika woman with ceremonial scarification.

MASAI WARRIOR of East Africa.

often treated like animals because to the foreigners, they resembled no human they had ever seen and were therefore frequently referred to as apes, gorillas and monkeys. ". . . I will make many people amazed at thee." An excerpt from the *New Funk & Wagnalls Encyclopedia (1952)* reads: "The Negro and Negroid peoples are sometimes said to represent a stage which is lower in evolutionary development than that of the white man, *and to be closely related to the anthropoid apes because they often have very long arms, protruding jaw, and a flat nose. These claims have no scientific justification . . .*" Dr. Na'im Akbar states that the 'big, wide noses' of black people were the result of "the need for more oxygen in the lungs because of the stifling heat of the sun that burns quite hot in most areas of Africa."

145

Says Akbar, "This climactic condition also contributed to black people having 'kinky' hair, to protect the head from the fierce heat of the sun." However, be that as it may, keep in mind that it was God who allowed these climactic, environmental changes that would ultimately effect the facial features, culminating into what is generally accepted today as typical Negroid features.

We read in God's Word that everything He made in the beginning was good but sin will distort and destroy even the most beautiful of anything. The prophet warned that the hereditary handsomeness that the Egyptians were noted for would no longer continue to be. The Egyptians would digress from the most attractive, most beautiful in the world, to the most unattractive. And what did God do instead? He commenced to glorify white beauty: blue eyes, blond hair, white complexion—features that had been present in the ancient world all along but had "paled" alongside— *why?* Simply because God, exercising His divine prerogative, had chosen to exalt and glorify Egyptian black beauty that it should stand out above all the others, ". . . nor any tree in the garden of God was like unto him in his beauty . . . so that all the trees of Eden, that were in the garden of God, *envied him* . . . To whom art thou thus like in glory and in greatness among the trees of Eden? . . . This is Pharaoh and all his multitude, saith the Lord God."

". . . *and their kings shall be horribly afraid for thee, when I shall brandish my sword before them* . . ." Kings, which represent overseers, slave masters and owners, shall, out of fear of you (horribly afraid) brandish my sword before them (wave my instrument of judgement). The instrument of judgement was most often 'the whip' which was applied, usually because of the fear brought about, not only by the fierce and bestial demeanor of the slaves, but also because of the grossness of their countenances. Struggling against heavy chains, anklets and other restraints only enhanced the impression of wild, uncivilized brutes, and undomesticated savages, which often resulted in their being treated like the animals they seemed to resemble. Appearing to be humans who had never been civilized (when in actuality, these people started civilization!) the slavemasters felt it their "Christian duty" to civilize these so-called "wild savages". First having to be subdued, then broken and tamed, domesticated, civilized then socialized. *What a comedown!* From the first in civilization to the last. From the very top to the very bottom. However, God had warned that if Pharaoh and Egypt did not repent and turn back to Him, this prophecy would fall upon all of Egypt and Ethiopia, including their descendants. Of course Pharaoh did not heed, therefore the prophecy was allowed to fall on the Egyptians and their descendants, black people of African descent.

"*. . . and they shall tremble at every moment, every man for his own life, in the day of thy fall.*" Roughly paraphrased: 'you shall live daily with the torment of fear of those who shall rule over you. Fear shall permeate practically every phase of your life: fear for the family unit, fear for life itself. The black man has ever lived in fear of the white man's power and influence over him, which has often been manifested in the form of racial prejudice, police brutality, and injustice in the judicial structure, as well as organized groups as the Ku Klux Klan and others. Many methods were employed towards "keeping the black man in his place". The *Funk & Wagnalls Encyclopedia (1952)* describes it this way: "Every Negro knew that if he were condemned in the court of white opinion as "uppity", disrespectful of white persons or assertive of rights against the wishes of white persons, or if he were arrested and awaiting trial for an offense against a white person, he might be seized by a mob, flogged, tarred and feathered, mutilated, or lynched without hope of rescue by other Negroes or the officers of the law, and without hope that his tormentors and murderers would be brought to justice, or if brought to trial, would be found guilty and punished. "*. . . and they shall tremble at every moment, every man for his own life . . .*" In America today, the black race's fear is no longer rooted basically in possible physical harm, although it can still happen, but there is yet a dread of white power that regulates jobs, job opportunities, promotions and advancements, education and business transactions. Black people have had to learn to live with the knowledge that, regardless of their education, abilities or skills, skin color will ultimately be the real deciding factor.

"The white government of South Africa is attempting to create four rigid colour-castes (Europeans, Asians, Africans. and Coloureds), to segregate them physically, and to perpetuate the economic and political privileges of the white minority at the expense of eighty percent of the population. In theory, apartheid aims to establish a "separate but equal" system, but in practice the indefinite maintenance of white supremacy is clearly the objective. Countless laws limit the nonwhite South Africans' rights to travel, own and occupy land, hold meetings, seek work, attend universities, enter public places, marry, vote, and indeed be present almost any place without the consent of the white authorities." (*Encyclopaedia Britannica 1983*).

> "For thus saith the Lord God; The sword of the king of Babylon shall come upon thee. By the swords of the mighty will I cause thy multitude to fall, the terrible of the nations, all of them: and they shall spoil the pomp of Egypt, and all the multitude thereof shall be destroyed."—Ezekiel 32:11–12

The conquest of Egypt by the king of Babylon was only the beginning of suffering and grief for the Egyptians. The armies of the mightiest nations (the terrible of the nations) shall descend upon Egypt with their weapons and its proud and imperious multitude shall fall at their hands. At this point, a brief historical outline is required to present the fulfillment of this portion of prophecy. In ancient times the Mediterranean region of Africa was of great importance. Rome gradually acquired this area in 149 B.C. After the dissolution of the Roman Empire came the invasion of the Arabs somewhere around the 6th century. Portugal, hoping to establish a trade route to India, began exploring the coasts of

Africa. A Portuguese, Bartholomew Diaz, was the first European to round the Cape of Good Hope in 1488. Portugal established many coastal stations to trade in the commodities for which Africa became famous—spices, ivory, gold, diamonds, and slaves. In the 18th and 19th centuries exploration of the exterior of Africa by well-known explorers as David Livingstone, Sir Henry Stanley, and others, commenced the really intense struggle between the powers for national and personal possessions in Africa, leaving the continent wide open to exploiters from outside. By 1912 these major world powers had partitioned Africa and only Liberia and Ethiopia were left independent. The division of the continent went like this: In the northwest, France acquired West Africa, Equatorial Africa, and portions of the Cameroons and established protectorates in Algeria, Morocco, and Tunisia. Other French territories were Somaliland. Togoland, Madagascar, and Reunion. The main group of British possessions, conquered for Queen and country, was in East and Southwest Africa which

included Egyptian Sudan, Uganda, Kenya Tanganyika, Zanzibar, Nyasaland, the Rhodesias, Bechuanaland, Basutoland, and Swaziland. Gambi, Sierra Leone, the Gold Coast, and Nigeria were Britain's possessions on the west coast. Portugal's African empire was made up of Guinea, Angola, and Mozambique, in addition to various enclaves and islands on the west coast. Belgium held the Belgian Congo, Ruanda and Urundi. The Spanish possessions were the smallest which included Spanish Guinea, Spanish Sahara, Ifni, and the protectorate of Spanish Morocco. Italy's empire included Libya, Eritrea, and Italian Somaliland. Germany's holdings included Togoland, a portion of the Cameroons, Southwest Africa, and German East Africa. ". . . *the terrible (mighty) of the nations, all of them.*"

". . . *and they shall spoil the pomp of Egypt . . .*" The word *pomp* meaning elaborate display; a striking and spectacular exhibition of wealth, grandeur and greatness. The golden age of Ancient Egypt produced the launching and execution of colossal undertakings and elaborate displays, not the least of which was the three Great Pyramids of Giza and the Step Pyramid, built by Imhotep, the first great structure of stone known in history. Visiting the country was like visiting the World Fair. Herodotus described Egypt as one of the greatest and most singular civilizations that has ever existed: "There is no country which possesses so many wonders nor any that has such a number of works which defy description." There was much pleasure to be found in the land of Egypt. Hebrews 11:24 states: "By faith Moses, when he was come to years, refused to be called the son of Pharaoh's daughter; choosing rather to suffer affliction with the people of God, *than to enjoy the pleasures of sin for a season*: Esteeming the reproach of Christ greater riches *than the treasures of Egypt . . .*" The fanfare surrounding the Egyptians' celebrations of their many gods in courts richly decorated and beautifully furnished, with dancing girls and the music of harp, flute and cymbals, was indeed a spectacle to behold. However, their funerary rituals, preparations and processionals, especially at

150

the deaths of one of their Pharaohs or other prominent officials, eventually became the most elaborate that the world has ever known. For rich and important persons, such as nobles, officials of the court, lord chamberlains and keepers of the crown, the elaborate process of funeral arrangements was long and costly, accompanied by elaborate processionals and much ado. A fine example of this is a painting from one of the ancient tombs in Thebes. The entourage of courtiers, attendants and followers made, literally, a spectacular parade, the like of which bears a striking resemblance to the famous funeral marches, led by black people in the city of New Orleans, Louisiana. These funeral processions surpassed

A feature common to the mural painting from Thebes shown above: the people shown are holding lotus flowers in their hands and apparently enjoying their perfume.

every other celebration the Egyptians were known for.

This ancient Egyptian practice of elaborate funeral celebrations was more or less passed down through the centuries by Egyptian descendants. An excerpt from Lerone Bennett states: "It was no less difficult to destroy the cultural heritage of Africans. This was manifested most notably in the widely reported "feasts and burials" of colonial blacks . . . One of these funerals was witnessed by Henry Knight who said it was customary in that day for black Virginians to "sing and dance and drink the dead to his new home, which some believe to be in old Guinea." The idea of a "big funeral", a custom that prevailed among most American blacks, even as late as the 1960s, has only recently begun to be phased out. A strong practice among much of the older generations was to "pay a lil' something" every month, for years and years on a burial policy, to insure that their funeral would be something really special. Sometimes there were hand-written special requests specifying certain arrangements to enhance their funeral day. No matter how poorly they had lived in life, it was important that in death, they should be "laid away real nice." The funeral parade of Dr. Martin Luther King that proceeded through the streets was very symbolic of the funeral processionals observed by the Ancient Egyptians thousands of years ago.

It was also a well-known fact that fabulous treasures and riches galore accompanied the bodies during these elaborate processionals and were buried with them in their famous tombs. In 1922, the sumptous furnishings of the tomb of King Tutankamen, who was not considered a ruler of real significance, indicates that the tombs of the really important Pharaohs originally must have been magnificent beyond imagination, making them the most elaborate ever known. ". . . and they shall *spoil the pomp of Egypt . . .*" The prophet declares that the spectacular exhibition of the traditional pomp and fanfare that accompanied the reputation of Egypt shall become a thing of the past.

> "I will destroy also all the beasts thereof from beside the great waters; neither shall the foot of man trouble them anymore, nor the hoofs of beasts trouble them. *Then will I make their waters deep, and cause their rivers to run like oil, saith the Lord God.*"—Ezekiel 32:13–14

Everything pertaining to the former state of Ancient Egypt would be vanquished and be no more. Beginning with the sword of Babylon, Egypt's multitude of people, including its domesticated animals (the beasts . . . from beside the great waters) shall be decreased. This lessening process continued until the slave trade was finally abolished around 1808.

"*Then will I make their waters deep* . . ." "Deep", meaning *to go underground*. There are many underground waters found in Africa's Sahara Desert, known as oases. They range in size from less than a square mile to those so large that several million date palms may be grown by the use of irrigation. ". . . and cause their rivers to run like oil . . ." The Hebrew translation means literally 'to cause their waters to settle'. Many of the oases of Africa are actually very large rivers that are 'locked in' underneath the ground (*I will make their waters deep*) and do not flow as rivers were intended to, but are confined to one place. A quote from the *1983 Encyclopaedia Britannica* in reference to the oases states that "In the desert proper sedentary occupation is confined to the oases, where irrigation permits limited cultivation . . . Cultivation is in small "gardens", maintained by a great expenditure of hand labour. Irrigation utilizes ephemeral streams in mountain areas, permanent pools, inclined underground tunnels dug to tap dispersed groundwater in the beds of oueds, springs and wells. Some shallow groundwaters are artesian, but generally water has to be lifted from wells by devices (a pivoted pole and bucket) worked by hand or animal. Most of the oases are watered by springs that are fed from underground water. Modern filling stations are situated at many of the oases, near the springs where camels still stop to drink and rest. The Western Sahara is almost entirely without rainfall or surface water but possess a number of underground rivers which flow from the Atlas Mountains and the mountains of the Tuareg Plateau. Occasionally the waters of these rivers find their way to the surface where plants grow freely. The Sahara total land area is 3,500,000 square miles of which 80,000 square miles consist of partially fertile oases." "*Then will I make their waters deep, and cause their rivers to run like oil* . . .*"

The Mystery Surrounding the Sahara Desert

"When I shall make the land of Egypt desolate, **and the country shall be destitute of that whereof it was full,** when I shall smite all them that dwell therein, then they shall know that I am the Lord."—Ezekiel 32:15

"When I shall make the land of Egypt desolate . . ." (deserted, dry, barren) Africa has about ten percent of the total population of the world, distributed over a land area representing about one fifth of the world's total land surface. Such desert areas as the Sahara and the Kalahari, however, reduce the amount of habitable land. Archaeologists have discovered that the Sahara was once fertile land before it became a desert barrier between the northern and southern parts of Africa. Long before recorded history, the Sahara was more widely occupied. Stone artifacts and rock pictures, widely scattered through regions now far too dry for occupation, reveal the former presence of man, together with big game animals including buffalo, giraffe, elephant and hippotamus, with forests, lakes and rivers that contained a permanent supply of fish. From hundreds of wall paintings dating back to 8000 B.C. prehistoric rock paintings in the central Sahara between Algeria and Libya indicate areas that were semi-jungle and giant trees and bunches of grapes almost two feet long. The paintings indicate that the Sahara once yielded luxurious vegetation with grazing grounds for domestic and wild animals with an abundant supply of water. The continent of Africa is almost bisected by the equator with about nine million square miles of its land lying within the tropics, making it an ideal climate for rich vegetation, an ideal cradle for the development of man. About 7000 years ago, according to scientific reports, Africa's climate was different from the climate there today. It is believed that it was once cool, with large well-watered forests and plains where fruits and vegetables abounded. In many areas, there was enough rainfall to allow grass and even trees to grow. It is said that hunters roamed the forests and grasslands in search of wild animals for food. Sheep, cattle and other livestock were raised on the grassy plains. As time passed, the climate of north Africa became drier and rivers that flowed there for many years eventually disappeared. The trees and grass withered and much of North Africa turned into a desert.

Although deserts existed on either side of the Nile River during

the Ancient Egyptians' time, history does not record that the desert was expanding. Therefore, no one knows definitely the exact time the Sahara began to expand, however, the drying up of the Sahara effected African life in many ways. Most of the people in the area moved out; some went north, some went south. Eventually, people on either side of the desert were separated from each other and could no longer communicate or exchange ideas.

When God allows certain conditions to exist, there is a basic reason why—which gives rise to this basic question: What catastrophic events could have taken place that would account for the Sahara Desert, an area as large as the United States of America, to simply dry up and turn into a desert? The answer to this question may never be quite clear, however, God's resolve to "make the land of Egypt desolate" can certainly account for the fact that the desert today is continuing to expand. It is basically the reason why scientists can't explain why it's happening, nor how it can be halted or even brought under control. It is, to scientists, a phenomenon that remains a scientific mystery, even in this day of high technology. As the Sahara continues to expand, a sixty mile border zone has to be used because sharp borderlines in the north and south cannot be drawn. Peculiarly, it is the *southern* border region that is said to contain "critical zones" because the desert is slowly but surely invading *sub-Sahara Africa!* *"When I shall make the land of Egypt desolate . . ."*

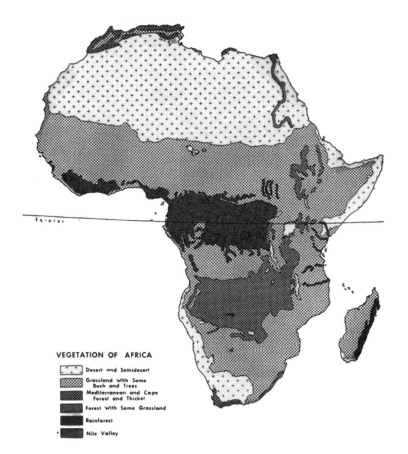

VEGETATION OF AFRICA

- Desert and Semidesert
- Grassland With Some Bush and Trees
- Mediterranean and Cape Forest and Thicket
- Forest With Some Grassland
- Rainforest
- Nile Valley

"... *and the country shall be destitute of that whereof it was full* ..."
The fulfillment of this prophecy is simply colossal! The prophet
declares that the whole country of Egypt (Africa) shall be stripped
of its wealth, "destitute of that whereof it was full . . .".and shall
become an easy prey to the invaders. According to *Vine's* interpretation 'destitute' means to be in lack or come short of. 'Full'
denotes having full measure; to be heavily laden with good things.
Africa, which is and always has been, the wealthiest continent on
the face of the earth, has the greatest bounty of natural resources
found anywhere in the world. The continent is so rich in natural
resources that it is often referred to as "The Golden Continent".
The prophet declared that the country shall one day "be destitute

156

(come short of) that whereof *it was full* (its bountiful natural resources).

Even in the ancient days Africa (Egypt) was known for its abundance of gold, just as it is today. Egypt was the great gold-mining and gold-exporting power; in fact, it was gold more than military success which sustained her empire and which made her the principal world power throughout the third quarter of the second milleneum B.C. We can indeed follow the influence of Egyptian gold from this intra-state correspondence written on clay tablets. This situation occurred when the Syrian state of Mitanni, violent foes of the Egyptians, was transformed by Egyptian subsidies into a buffer-state against the expanding Hittites further north. Thus we have King Tushratta of Mitanni, writing to Pharaoh Amenophis III: "My brother pray send gold in very great quantities such as cannot be counted. My brother please send me that. And my brother please send me more gold than my father

157

got from you. For in the land of my brother, is not gold as plentiful as the dust upon the ground?"

In a statement from Paul Johnson's book: "Egypt became a major gold producing state in the Old Kingdom and remained one for 1,500 years—with interruptions when the state broke down. During the New Kingdom, the production of gold increased steadily as mining became more extensive and new fields were developed." After visiting Egypt in 450 B.C. Herodotus, the Greek historian reported: "The furthest inhabited country towards the southwest is Ethiopia. Here gold is found in great abundance . . ."

An astronomer, Al Fazari, who wrote between 788–793 A.D. on the main kingdoms of the world, referred to Ghana as a land of gold with many gold mines. Another writer, Ibn Kawoala, who visited Ghana between 901–902, said that the king of Ghana was the richest in the world because of his abundance of gold. Al Masudi wrote *The Golden Prairies* and described Ghana as a land where gold was visible in the ground.

The measure of the incredible wealth of Egypt can be assessed from the account of the tomb of King Tutankamen, "Tut" for short, which was discovered by Howard Carter in 1922: "His burial chambers were in reality a suite of four rooms. Two of these were crowded with chariots, fine furniture, curious looking boxes, artistically painted chests, and inlaid coffers filled with fine linens and silks and innumerable changes of every kind of rich clothing known to the royalty of that day. One elaborately decorated robe had on it 50,000 beads, and the entire surface of the sandals worn by the sentinels at the doorway was covered with pure gold decorations. Carter and his staff spent three weeks inspecting the many objects found in only one of these beautifully painted wooden chests, the outside of which he said, 'far surpassed anything of the kind that Egypt had produced.' There were many chests of gems and jewels, fine bronze work, plaques of pearl, and gold, gold, gold almost everywhere.

The third room was the 'treasure room', whose doorway was guarded by an ebony and gold figure of the jackal god Anubis, which crouched on top of a beautiful shrine. Behind him were shrines, model boats, another chariot and a tier of wooden coffers, studded with gold and inlaid with faience. A large shrine-shaped chest was surmounted by a cornice of sacred cobras, inlaid with gold. When this was dismantled, a beautiful chest of transparent alabaster appeared, covered over with a linen pall. Within this beautiful chest were four miniature inlaid gold coffins which contained the viscera of the king. This canoptic shrine not only represented the highest attainment of the art of the Egyptian goldsmith and jeweler, but was a reminder of the beautiful and ornate Ark of the Covenant made more than a century before at Mount Sinai by Moses and the Hebrew artisans.

The Tomb Room was still more gorgeous. There were four shrines, one within the other, each similar in design and even more brilliant in workmanship. After unsealing and unbolting the last door, there was revealed an immense yellow quartzite sarcophagus, intact, just as the pious hands had left it. It was covered with religious inscriptions and pictures, and topped with a beautiful rose-granite lid. When the 2500 pound lid was raised, and a linen shroud removed, there was revealed a magnificent golden effigy of the young king, filling the whole interior of the sarcophagus. The arms were crossed on the breast, and the hands held the golden flail and scepter (rod and staff); both adorned with lapis lazuli. This gorgeous coffin enclosed a second, also mummiform and of equal beauty with the first. Within the second was a third and last, of solid gold and adorned with jewels. This last mummiform casket weighed some 1800 pounds and its monetary value was more than one million dollars.

When the last lid was raised by its handles, the mummy of the king lay disclosed. Over his face was a gold portrait of the king, and about his mummified body were 143 objects—mostly gold or precious jewels. What a burial, and what enormous wealth!

Paul Johnson relates: "The wealth deliberately deposited in these royal tombs must have been incalculable. In accordance with the immortality theory, all the artifacts used were if possible

159

of the most costly and durable material. Gold, in particular, was the substance of the gods, and used whenever appropriate. It was also their flesh—so that the masks and mummy-covers of royalty were of solid gold." Archaeologists estimate that many more are still preserved in undiscovered tombs and burial places. The discovery,

The outer coffin of Tutankhamnun from the Valley of the Kings, Thebes.

from time to time, of the embalmed body of an ancient Pharaoh constitutes a major archaeological find.

"... *and the country shall be destitute of that whereof it was full* ..." Because of the annual overflowing of the Nile River, the Egyptians were always assured of a bountiful harvest, from one century to the other, therefore, there was hardly ever a shortage of food. Today, by contrast, starvation prevails in many areas of the land. As a matter of fact, Africa's situation today could be typed as an enigma, in view of the fact that the continent is yet considered the richest in the world, yet so poor in living standards, being forced to beg and depend on the charity of other nations. Is there a reason for this puzzling situation? Indeed there is.

During the years of slavery trade Africa suffered from the constant and systematic plunder of her material wealth and the selling of her ablest and fittest sons and daughters. Europeans have been taking African wealth out of the country for over 300 years. After the staking of claims and the carving-up of colonies, commonly referred to as the Berlin Conference of 1884–85, began the discovery and exploitation of valuable African resources and minerals (gold, diamonds) and valuable export crops (coca, coffee, palm oil, cotton, tea) in addition to the setting up of industrial and administrative cities and ports with their ensuing mills and factories. In view of the fact that Africa was esteemed to be merely a country full of ignorant natives, no rent, compensation or permission was required to acquire access to this tremendous wealth. Did the occupants of the continent attempt to dissuade the invaders and prevent the takeover of their land? Indeed, they did. History, in the form of books, newspapers and movies, to name a few, bear witness to the courage of the African natives as they fought unflinchingly against unfamiliar modern weapons, in their efforts to retain their continent. When the Europeans began to take over Africa, farming, transportation and communication were very primitive as was practically everything that pertained to the continent (Long-distance messages were carried by drums).

European depiction of a clash between British troops and Bantu warriors in the eastern frontier region of Cape Colony, South Africa, in 1851.

Even today almost all Africans are small-scale farmers who have traditionally relied on simple tools and techniques, growing just enough to feed the immediate family. As a result, much of the continent's rich natural resources were not being used. In their search for the virgin wealth of the land, the Europeans started plantations and opened mines to obtain the raw materials needed for their factories and built roads and railroads to transport the farm crops, trees and other valuable mineral wealth out of Africa. To the Europeans, Africa was simply a storehouse of raw materials to be used for their own benefit. In the meantime, the African people themselves reaped the benefit of none of their own resources and have, to this day, remained very poor. It is this very same situation that the prophet Ezekiel warned would come to pass, eventually, if there was no repentance and a turning back to God: ". . . and the country shall be destitute of that whereof it was full . . ." In other words, "You shall one day be made destitute (drained, depleted and poor) of that whereof you have much (its bounty of natural resources).

It is reported that one day, in 1866, a farmer's child was walking along the banks of the Orange River in South Africa, and found a strange pebble. People wondered what it was and to their surprise and amazement, learned that it was a diamond worth $2,500! Two years later a shepherd boy in South Africa found another diamond. This one was worth $55,000! The discovery of diamonds in South Africa attracted thousands of treasure seekers. They soon began to dig diamond mines and today nearly all the world's diamonds are mined in Africa, particularly in South Africa. The great majority of the workers hired to work these mines are the Africans themselves. However, none of the enormous profits from this enterprise goes to the native Africans.

Africa is often mistakenly looked upon as a "poor and starving nation" when, ironically, according to its abundant, natural resources it is the richest continent in the world. Practically every section of Africa has at least four to five valuable resources of some kind. So far, all of the development of these resources have come from outside of Africa. Foreigners, chiefly Europeans, have invested their capital in African possessions and profits have gone largely out of the country to the investors. In recent years, a resentment has built up against this condition by the native Africans whose feeling for Pan-Africanism—Africa for the Africans—is awakening throughout the enormous continent.

Although most of Africa today is governed by native Africans, Europeans for purely financial reasons, have not completely loosed their hold on the continent. The fruit of its labor is still enjoyed mainly by Europeans while the native people go hungry and many die of starvation. The people are indeed "destitute of that whereof it was full". To better understand the situation and the fulfillment of the prophecy, it is necessary to point out the abundance (*fullness*) of the continent's riches, country by country.

Diamonds and gold are the minerals most people think of in connection with Africa, however, these two are only the tip of the iceberg. The following statistics (found commonly in any

Encyclopedia Britannica or *The World Almanac and Book of Facts*) details why Africa's mineral wealth and other resources place it in the category of *World's Richest Continent*. Africa has about one third of the world's reserves of *bauxite*, an ore used to make aluminum. One half of the world reserves of *cobalt* can be found in Zaire where an estimated 1,300,000 tons of cobalt metal are located with other deposits in Morocco. The major concentrations of *bryllium* are in Madagascar, Mozambique, Zaire and Zimbabwe. Almost the entire world reserve of *chromium* is found in southern Africa and parts of west and northeast Africa. *Manganese* reserves are considerable. In South Africa reserves of about 800,000,000 tons of contained *manganese* are found in the Kalahari Manganese Field and elsewhere in Gabon and Ghana. There are also deposits of *vanadium*, a rare element used to toughen steel and to increase its shock resistance. Africa contains a major share of world reserves of *tantalum* (70%) with reserves located in Zaire, Nigeria and Kenya. One of Africa's many sources of *zirconium* (a metallic element chemically resembling *titanium*) is in Nigeria. Other reserves are contained on the Senegal coast, on the east coast of South Africa, Madagascar, Sierra Leone and in the Nile Delta.

Another rare metal which Africa contains a majority of world reserves is *germanium*, concentrated in Zaire and Namibia. There are also large deposits of *lithium*: the largest deposits are found in Zaire. South Africa has the most important deposit of *platinum*, amounting to an estimated 450,000,000 troy ounces. Zaire has the world's chief source of *radium*, located in the *uranium* ores of the Shinkolobwe-Kasaolo area.

Africa's reserves of minerals used as ferroalloys in the steel industry are even more striking than its vast share of world iron ore reserves. This is particularly true of *chromium*. Almost the entire world reserve of *chromium* is found in southern, western and northeastern Africa.

Most of Africa's *copper* is contained in the Central African Copperbelt. In the late 1970s Zambia was estimated to have

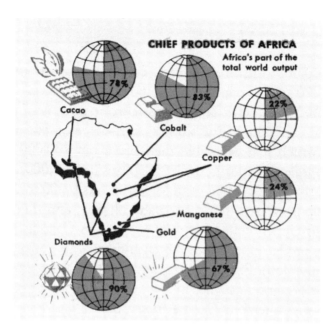

CHIEF PRODUCTS OF AFRICA

Africa's part of the total world output

Cacao 78%

Cobalt 83%

Copper 22%

Manganese 24%

Gold 67%

Diamonds 90%

Chief Products of Africa

36,000,000 tons and Zaire 26,000,000 tons of contained *copper*, out of a total for African reserves of almost 76,000,000 tons. Outside the *copper* belt a number of countries have lesser but still significant reserves of *copper*. Botswana also has 530,000 tons of *copper* metal reserves while Mauritania has the largest reserves of West Africa, 740,000 tons. In east Africa Uganda has a reserve of more than 200,000 tons, just to name a few.

Although it is difficult to consider Africa's reserves of *lead* and *zinc* separately, its *lead* ores are considerably more widespread. Total *lead* reserves are about 1,000,000,000 tons. North Africa is the largest traditional producing region. Reserves of *zinc* are estimated at 16,500,000; they are located along the Moroccan-Algerian frontier, also in the *copper* belt of Zaire, in Nigeria, in Zambia, and Namibia.

North Africa has been a traditional exporter of phosphates and West Africa has large reserves. Morocco and Western Sahara together have the vast reserves of 20,000,000,000 tons of *phosphate*. The Rio de Oro region in Western Sahara contains huge deposits. Algeria and Tunisia together have a further

165

12,000,000,000 tons. To the east, Egyptian reserves total about 660,000,000 tons. Togo has about 60,000,000 tons and Senegal 140,000,000 tons. The Thies deposit in Senegal is of particular interest in constituting the world's only source of *aluminum phosphate*, of which it is estimated there are about 100,000,000 tons. Other *phosphate* deposits occur in Tanzania (10,000,000 tons) Uganda (180,000,000 tons) and Malawi (18,000,000 tons).

Granite is located in Morocco and Nigeria, and there are vast reserves in Upper Volta. *Quartzite* is found in Uganda and Zaire. *Dolerite* is produced in South Africa and *basalt* in Senegal. *Marble* is found in Mali, Togo, Nigeria, and South Africa. *Limestone* is important because of its use in the cement industry, and deposits are fairly widespread. In West Africa a belt of *limestone* runs from the central African Republic to the Atlantic coasts, with major outcrops in northern Nigeria, Upper Volta, and Mali. Elsewhere there are deposits in Togo and Ghana. East African deposits include those in Kenya, Tanzania, Uganda, Zambia, and South Africa. North Africa has major reserves of *gypsum* on the Mediterranean coast and along the Gulf of Suez and the Red Sea. Somalia has a reserve of 30,000,000 tons—one of the largest

A chief of the Yacouba tribe, refugees from Liberia, helps distribute rice.

known deposits.

It is pointed out that most sections of Africa have at least two to three valuable export products. The so-called *dual-mandate* purposed by the Europeans, based on 'Using Africa's Resources For Africa's Own Development' has proved over the years, to be only empty words. The real truth here is that nearly all of the minerals that are dug out of African soil are shipped to countries in other parts of the world. No type of compensation has ever been offered in exchange for these valuable resources, or even expected, since the properties of Africa belong mainly to the investors. The technology and development that was brought into Africa by Europeans was not to 'Use Africa's Resources for Africa's Own Development' but instead, to take African wealth out of the country and heartlessly leave behind hunger, starvation and even death. Trains carrying loads of raw materials out of Africa (gold, diamonds, phosphate, sugar, copper) are not destined for countries within Africa's own land to be deposited at Africa's own steel mills and factories (which Africans do not own anyway) but instead they are shipped to mostly European markets. Nowhere else in the world has such shameful exploitation of a country taken place, except in Africa. *Why?* The world has been aware of these operations taking place for over 300 years yet never has there been a universal outcry against such unfair exploitation. *Why?* The reason, whether anyone wants to believe it or not, is totally spiritual, based on the prophecy levied against our forebears, the Ancient Egyptians, thousands of years ago: "And I will . . . *sell the land* into the hand of the wicked: *and I will make the land waste, and all that is therein, by the hand of strangers:* I, the Lord have spoken it . . . *and the country shall be destitute of that whereof it was full* . . . then shall they know that I am the Lord." It was not His will—nor His intention that any should come to the aid of Egypt, that His word might be fulfilled: "I have therefore delivered him into the hand of the mighty one of the heathen; he shall surely deal with him . . . *and strangers, the terrible of the nations, have cut him off, and have left him*: upon the mountains and in all the valleys . . . *and all the people of the earth are gone down from his shadow, and have left him.*"

Africa is the wealthiest continent on the face of the earth, yet forced to accept charity from other nations: possessing the greatest bounty of resources found anywhere, yet forced to buy goods from other nations rather than manufacturing her own. In the words of Ali A. Mazrui: *"Producing what they do not use, and using what they do not produce."* Africa is a treasure-house of minerals, producing more than two-thirds of the world's *gold*, also about two-thirds of the world's *cobalt*. It also provides about one-third of the world's *antimony*, a metal used to harden other metals and about one-fourth of the world's *manganese*, an ingredient used in making certain kinds of steel. About one-fourth of the world's *copper* is manufactured there and a large amount of *uranium* comes out of African mines. Libya and Algeria in North Africa (owned by the Arabs) are among the world's leading producers of *petroleum*. The discovery of *petroleum* in Africa influenced the growth of imports. Between 1938 and 1978, total exports increased in value from $1,000,000,000 to $53,000,000,000. Other factors include the discoveries of much-in-demand minerals such as *diamonds, gold and uranium ore.* In the mid-1970s the *petroleum* industry was very unevenly distributed with about half of mineral earnings coming from North Africa (Arabs) alone and about 30 percent from South Africa. During the late 1970s about 23 of Africa's 50 countries had at least one *petroleum* refinery and was producing 65,000,000 tons per year, not including South Africa. Today the number has increased tremendously. *Coal, oil,* and rich beds of *phosphate* have already been discovered in the rocky regions of the Sahara. A quote from the *Encyclopedia Britannica:* "In metallic minerals, major iron-ore reserves have been found, particularly at Gara-Djebilet, Algeria, southwest of Tindouf, where reserves are estimated to approach 1,500,000,000 metric tons, and at Kediet Ijill in Western Mauritania, where reserves are also substantial.

Near Akjoujy, in Mauritania lie an estimated 27,000,000 tons of *copper ore*; extensive *manganese* deposits occur at Djebel Guettara, south of Bechar, Algeria; and in the older crystalline rocks of the Ahaggar, Air, Tibesti, and Lglab regions have been found a long list of metals, including *tin, nickel, chromium, zinc, lead, cobalt, silver, gold, platinum molybdenum* (a metallic element used in strengthening steel), *wolfram* (used as a source of tungsten), *thorium* (a radioactive metallic element) and *uranium*."

Because Africa has so many rich mineral deposits, mining is important in several parts of the continent. However, the so-called 'technology needed for the development of African resources' is clearly based upon the various types of industries and businesses that deal strictly with removing the rich raw materials from the continent. When the Europeans first began to take over Africa they paid very low wages to the African labourers ($2.50 a day) and kept the profits they made for themselves. In the meantime, the African people reaped the benefit of none of their own resources and remained very poor. The yearly per capita income was $50-$150, hardly justifying the exchange of African resources for Western technology. Factories in the U. S. and Europe need the minerals found in Africa and for that reason, Europeans and Americans spend billions of dollars to establish mines there.

Another most important resource in Africa is waterpower. The continent has enough waterpower to produce more than one third of the world's hydro-electricity. Because of the handicap of natural cataracts, and the many hard to reach places where the water is located, Africa has only in recent years begun to develop more of its waterpower. Nevertheless, the use of electric energy in Africa has grown and is growing at a spectacular rate. Several of the great rivers have been harnessed to provide power for the many foreign-owned petroleum industries and areas that depend totally upon the abundance of natural mineral resources. Large dams such as the Kariba Dam on the Zambezi River, the Aswan High Dam on the Nile, the Askosombo Dam on the Volta River in Ghana and the

Owen Falls Dam have been constructed and more are envisaged. Beginning from 1937 to 1939, electric energy production increased twenty-five times— from 6,500,000,000 kilowatt hours to 168,000,000,000, mostly because of the establishment of large hydroelectric plants that have successfully cultivated the water resources in the areas of Africa where the waters, though abundantly plentiful, are yet inconveniently located. The largest consumption, naturally, is in the mining areas, coastal areas and large urban centers where European and Asian industrial activities are the greatest. The hydro-electric resources of Africa represent 3,140,000,000,000 kilowatt hours. Geothermal energy is also a potentially major source of electric energy, especially in East Africa where many active volcanoes and hot springs are associated with the Great Rift Valley.

The vast forests of Africa provide other valuable natural resource. In 1979 there was an estimated 1,700,000,000 acres of forests and woodlands. The wood from hardwood trees, such as the ebony and the mahogany, is shipped to mills and factories in other parts of the world where it is used to make lumber, furniture and other products, after all, the average native of Africa has little or no use at all for these fine trees that are so highly valued elsewhere in the world, for his little hut is made up entirely of grasses, weeds and hay. Other valuable trees are the oil palms rubber trees and cacao. Seeds from the cacao are used in making cocoa and chocolate. Although a number of small paper mills are established in West, Central and East Africa, the pulp and paper industry is concentrated in North Africa and southern Africa. The African output of wood pulp amounted to about 1,300,000 tons in 1979, 60 percent of which was exported mainly to Europe. The bulk of the output of all paper products was directed to national markets. ". . . and I will make the land waste, and all that is therein, by the hand of strangers . . . and the land shall be destitute of that whereof it was full . . ."

Because of inadequate diet, many Africans are constantly in

poor health and suffering with diseases such as tuberculosis, malaria, and sleeping sickness, causing many deaths among the people. Ironically, the lack of food in most areas is not because there is a lack of food being grown in those areas. On the contrary. For instance, there are many different kinds of fish in the oceans and seas that surround the huge continent of Africa. Fishermen from Morocco catch tuna, sardines and other fish off the country's Atlantic coast. Southwest of the coast are lobster, whitefish, and other kinds of seafoods. In 1979 alone, Africa's total catch of fresh and saltwater fish was 4,800,000 tons. The countries that con-tributed to this total besides South Africa were: Nigeria. Tanzania, Namibia, Senegal, Ghana, Uganda, Egypt, Zaire, Chad, Angola, Mali, Ivory Coast, Cameroon and Malawi. Amazingly, a large number of these countries are familiar to the American public because they are the very same countries that have pleaded over the years for food donations and money for the starving. However, it must be kept in mind that although most of the governments of the countries of Africa are now controlled by the African native people, the lands are basically owned and controlled by foreigners, Europeans in particular.

The 1983 *Encyclopedia Britannica* (Vol. 9, pg. 1186) gives this very candid observation concerning the financial future of the Ivory Coast of Africa: "Its government gave French capitalists a free hand, and they have responded with investments that brought about a spectacular economic expansion. A new local social class is taking its part of the profits and is expecting to gain more from the completion of existing projects. About the future, however, several questions remain to be answered. One is whether the local beneficiaries of this manna will be willing, or capable, of reinvesting it locally. So far they have taken no positive step in this direction, though they were expected to do so and thus to stimulate an even greater growth in the 1970s.

Another question is whether the country will ever be able to stop the *transfer abroad of its surplus and thus make itself economically independent.* According to leading authorities, the Ivory Coast is now *as dependent on foreign aid as it has been for years*, and *transfers of profit abroad* represent an enormous percentage of the national product. These questions must be answered in a positive way if the people of the Ivory Coast are to be allowed to enjoy the fruits of their exertions." . . . *and I will sell the land into the hand of the wicked* . . .

The majority of the countries in Africa has a very large share of the world's mineral resources. *Sierra Leone's* rich fields are worked for diamonds, which is one of its most valuable exports. For years smugglers drained Sierra Leone of more than $30,000,000 worth of diamonds every year, before being brought under control. *Guinea's* major mineral resource is *bauxite* and is believed to have the richest *bauxite* reserves in the world. An *aluminum* plant built at Kimbo, started production in 1960. It is owned jointly by U.S., French, British and West German firms. *Gold* and *diamonds* are also mined in Guinea. The town of Lubumbashi, in the Republic of *Zaire*, is another rich *copper* mining region (56% of world reserves in 1970s). *Copper* is Zambia's most important export product (95% of world s reserves in 1970). About a hundred miles from Lubumbashi is a large open-pit mine that produces *uranium* for atomic energy plants in the U.S. Lubumbashi produced a good supply of *copper* for world export., and the natives that were civilized were kept busy at the mines and smelting works.

For years the Congo was the world's principal source of *radium*, a radioactive element highly valued in medicine for the treatment of tumors. Another valuable mineral of the Congo is *thorium* and *uranium* which are important in the production of atomic energy. Since the fields of Katanga yield both, the Congo should, as it has done until now, continue to furnish a large portion of the raw materials that are needed for atomic research. In 1965, in the Congo Basin, a belt of valuable mines, 200 miles long, extended through the highlands. In the southern and eastern highlands are *gold, uranium, platinum,* and *coal.*

The sands of the Kasai River, a major tributary of the Congo, yield most of the world's *diamond* supply. Although the value of South Africa's *diamond* production is far greater, most Congo *diamonds* which are of an imperfect shape, are also valuable and are used for industrial purposes. The *diamond*, whether it is of gem quality or not, is the hardest substance known to man. They expand only the tiniest fraction when they are heated and are therefore especially long-wearing and accurate when used as bearings in delicate instruments. Granite is cut with saws that have diamonds set in their teeth. Oil well drills tipped with industrial *diamonds* bore through shelves of rock that resist all other cutting tools.

A quote from the 1983 *Encyclopedia Britannica:* ". . . industrial *diamonds* are most closely associated with Africa. The continent contains about 95 percent of the total Western-world reserves. The stones are found in a number of major belts south of the Sahara. The principal known reserves of *diamonds* in their primary form (in the rough) are in the South African Vaal Belt. Elsewhere in Africa, primary deposits are found in Tanzania, Botswana, and Lesotho.

Another major belt of diamondiferous rocks encircles the Congo Basin and includes the world's largest deposit, located in Zaire, which contains the majority of Western reserves of industrial diamonds. The same belt has secondary deposits that occur elsewhere in that country, as well as in the Central African Republic and Angola. In West Africa known reserves are located primarily in alluvial gravel fields. They are found in Sierra Leone, Guinea, Ivory Coast, Liberia and Ghana."

Of the many major *diamond* deposits in Africa, one major deposit, located in southwest Africa, renamed Namibia, consists almost entirely of gem *diamonds.* "There is no other gem mineral in Africa of comparable importance to these *diamond* reserves. Deposits of a number of such stones are found, however, especially

173

in Southern Africa and East Africa, where *diamond* fields contain *beryl, garnets, amethysts, rose quartz, topaz, opal, jasper, emeralds* and other stones. Madagascar contains a large deposit of *garnet . . . agate* is particularly associated with the volcanic areas of east and south Africa, . . . while *sapphires* are found with diamonds in Ghana." (*Encyclopedia Britannica*).

"*. . . and the country shall be destitute of that whereof it was full . . .*" The "fullness" of the continent of Africa, speaking in reference to Africa's bountiful natural resources, has indeed continued to be depleted (destitute), as prophesied, over the past three centuries, thanks to the outside technology of European and Asian countries. Understandably, these resources could not have been developed without European capital and technology. This too, was a fulfillment of the prophecy: "*. . . and I will make the land waste, and all that is therein, by the hand of strangers . . .*"

Europeans did not become interested in "darkest Africa" until the 15th and 16th centuries when Portuguese traders, on their way from Europe to the Orient, realized that towns could be established on the African coast as way stations. For almost a hundred years the Portuguese were the major explorers of the coast of Africa and the first to trade in the commodities for which Africa became famous—spices, ivory, gold, diamonds and slaves. As early as 1441 the Portuguese transported the first African slaves to Portugal, beginning the European—and later American—entrance into that most tragic of all businesses: slavery. The Dutch, English and French began to compete with the Portuguese in the 16th and 17th centuries. In the 18th and 19th century exploration of the interior of Africa by explorers exposed the continent's great natural wealth, which could be obtained and exploited simply by the founding of colonies. Many of the journeys of the explorers were paid for by men or companies seeking wealth in Africa. "*. . . and the country shall be destitute of that whereof it was full . . .*"

The presence of Europeans, Asians and other foreign countries in Africa today is primarily because of the "*full*-ness" of the continent, its wealth of minerals and other natural resources. Most Europeans in Africa live in the far north or the far south. There are French, English, Dutch, Spanish, Portuguese, German and Belgian settlers who mostly own and manage mines, plantations, manufacturing companies, mills and other types of industry that exploit the natural resources to the tune of billions of dollars a year. As stated before, this is possible because practically every section of Africa has at least two to three valuable export products. Another casual glance in the *Encyclopedia Britannica 1986 Book Of The Year* will reveal this fact. Take Tanzania, for example: "*diamonds* and *salt* are important . . . The Nyanzian rocks south and east of Lake Victoria are *gold bearing*; to the west, *tin* and *tungsten* deposits have been located. *Mica* is found in central and eastern Tanzania. In the south, deposits of *lead, copper, silver* and *gold* have been found. In the southwest, large quantities of *coal* and *iron* have been proved. In several of the volcanic pipes (eruptive passages of volcanoes) *diamonds* are to be found. Deposits of *limestone, gypsum, salt, kaolin (china clay) and rock phosphate* occur in the coastal and lake regions.

Tanzania has substantial biological resources. The forests contain tropical hardwoods, such as *mahogany* and *teak; softwoods* are found in mountain areas. The exploitation of coastal fisheries has barely begun. The ample energy resources of Tanzania include quantities of *charcoal* and *firewood*, large resources of *coal* in the south (amounting to more than 304,000,000 tons) and adequate waterpower.

Gold occurs along the Niger and its tributaries, and *diamonds* occur in the gravels of the Makona River tributaries. The southeastern rain forests contain valuable *hardwoods*. Ghana, formerly known as *The Gold Coast*, has a wide range of minerals but only a few major ones such as *gold, diamonds, manganese* and *bauxite*, have been exploited. The *gold* industry in Ghana is the oldest with an unbroken history dating from the 15th century. There are reserves of *limestone* and *iron ore*, and an *iron ore* mine at

175

Opon-Mansi was being developed in the early 1980s. In 1970 *oil* was discovered. In 1974 there were discoveries of substantial amounts of *natural gas*. The most important of the biological resources is *cocoa*, of which Ghana is a leading world producer. The annual output of *cocoa* varies from 250,000 to 400,000 tons, and *cocoa* provides up to 3/4 of the country's total revenue from exports. The same goes for Gabon with major resources of *gold*, *manganese* and *uranium*; Mozambique with resources of *limestone*, *copper* and *garnet*; Cameroon with *aluminum, gold, limestone and petroleum*; Zaire with *copper, zinc, cobalt, manganese, tin, silver, gold, gem diamonds and industrial diamonds*; Zambia with *copper, gold, zinc, lead, and cobalt*; Zimbabwe with *gold* and *copper*; just to name a few. Is there any wonder the continent is often referred to as "God's Treasure Chest"?

"... the country shall be destitute *of that whereof it was full* ..." The 1991 Persian Gulf War fought in Saudi Arabia was not the first war fought explicitly for resources. That type of war started around 1884 when the intense rivalry of the nations of Europe for African territory threatened to trigger pandemonium. As a result, a conference was called (The Berlin Conference of 1884–1885) where the major world powers defined the boundaries of their various African holdings and laid down certain laws, among which was the rule that when a power acquired new territory in Africa, it must notify the other powers.

Much bloodshed ensued from that point on, as the native Africans, in their futile attempts to halt the invasion of the foreigners, fougnt boldly and courageously to retain their land. Sadly, it is a war that has continued through the centuries. According to the *Universal Standard Encyclopedia*: "British authority in Kenya was challenged during 1952 by the Mau Mau (Hidden ones), a secret terrorist cult of native tribesmen who had sworn to expel all whites from the colony. By the end of October Mau Mau members had murdered more than fifty white colonists and pro-British natives. The cult's activities continued in 1953, 1954 and 1955,

176

despite severe reprisals, including frequent mass executions of convicted offenders. By the end of January, 1955, Mau Mau tribesmen killed in skirmishes with government forces totaled more than 7800."

The whites even fought with one another over possession of rich African lands. In the Boer War the British fought with the Boers (Dutch settlers) from 1899 to 1902 in an attempt to settle boundary disputes. Great Britain won out over the Dutch and in 1910 unified the Transvaal, the Orange Free State, the Cape of Good Hope Colony and Natal. These states, rich in diamonds and gold became a dominion of the British Commonwealth of Nations, better known as the Union of South Africa. British views in South Africa, however, remained influential until in 1948 when the Nationalist Party, backed by the South African 'Africaners' (white settlers), defeated the British-supported United Party at the polls. In 1961 South Africa left the Commonwealth of Great Britain and became a Republic, making itself a free state, virtually self-governing, favoring a policy of white supremacy.

'. . . and I will sell the land into the hand of the wicked . . .' There are many people, even most African Americans, who do not fully understand the real reason why the foreigners in Africa, who are clearly the minority, refuse to allow the indigenous natives to rule their own land. The bountiful riches of the continent and the easy acquisition of the land has, for many, many years made Africa and its native people easy pickings for any who were looking to make themselves rich. This in spite of the fact that much of Africa's climate is not favorable to most foreigners who choose to live there, hence the reason they are mainly found residing in the extreme north of the continent (near the Mediteranean Coast) or in the extreme south. The Republic of South Africa is a prime example. This small excerpt, taken from the '83 *Encyclopedia Britannica* states: "South Africa's location, almost entirely south of the Tropic of Capricorn and within temperate climactic zones, *contributed to European settlement on a scale unknown elsewhere in Africa.*"

Diamond mining in South Africa

Although the country is far enough away from the equator to have a milder climate than other areas, this does not mean that ideal conditions exist. When the first European settlers arrived in the 17th century, South Africa had an unbelievable wealth of animal life, including lions, elephants, rhinoceros, and a variety of antelopes. Today, however, such wildlife exists only in the most marginal areas, such as the Kalahari. Except for the southwestern corner, the entire western half is dry. Most of the west coastal section is a true desert, called the Namib Desert. The rest is a semi-desert known as the Kalahari. The eastern section normally has enough rainfall for crops, but some parts are subject to severe and frequent drought. Farmers are constantly faced with the problem of a water shortage; water for irrigation is limited. Some of the western portion does not even have enough rainfall to provide pasture for livestock. In many places soils are sandy and poor in plant foods. Other parts are too rugged to be used for growing crops or even for grazing. Yet there are more Europeans living in South Africa than in any other part of the continent. The main reason being, of course, that many rich mineral deposits are found there.

178

Minerals are South Africa's most valuable resource. Kimberly and Johannesburg are the two principal cities in South Africa from the point of view of wealth and industry. Kimberly is noted for its diamonds and Johannesburg lies in the richest gold belt in the world. Diamonds, many pure enough to be used as gem stones, were first found near Kimberly in 1870. For many years after this discovery, South Africa was the world's leading diamond-producing country, and remains a leading source of gem quality stones.

A spectacular gold strike was made in 1886 when the world's largest deposit of ore was discovered near the present city of Johannesburg. This deposit, called the Witwatersrand, or The Rand, makes South Africa the greatest gold-producing country in the world, producing more gold than any other gold-mining region in the world. In the gold mines, shafts several thousand feet deep have been sunk in the earth, and galleries have been driven out in all directions at the bottom in the search for gold, of which there seems to be a never-ending supply. Gold reserves of 530,000,000 troy ounces probably constitute about one half of the world total.

Apart from gold and diamonds, there are nearly 70 other types of exploitable minerals in South Africa. The largest deposits of coal on the continent are in South Africa, with 65,000,000,000 tons. The principal sources of cadmium are in South Africa and, in addition, the Republic is said to be one of the world's seven major uranium provinces. Because mineral resources are extensive, the bases of South Africa's economy consists of mining and manufacturing. This statement from the *Encyclopedia Britannica*: "Diamonds and gold are the best known and historically the most important minerals (in South Africa), but there are many others of growing importance, including copper, iron ore, manganese, asbestos, chrome, silver, beryllium, antimony, tin, platinum and some resources have yet to be exploited . . . Gold accounts for 60 percent of total mineral sales. Gold is produced in three main areas—the Witwatersrand, which includes Johannesburg; the Far

West Rand and Klerksdorp fields; and the Orange Free State around Odendaalsrus . . . There is also diamond production in the Orange Free State and the Transvaal Production in 1979 was 8,384,000 caarats—a 20 percent increase from 1971." According to the *1989 World Almanac*, South Africa's Gross National Production (GNP) for the year of 1985 alone totaled a whopping $112,000,000,000!

Understandably, the Europeans, who left their own native land to settle permanently in Africa, have continuously refused for over 300 years to relinquish their hold on the continent. After, all, would it make sense, otherwise, that 5 million whites would be so willing to live among 22 million blacks (whom they clearly detest), except there be a strong reason for it?

Let's review the prophecy again: "And I will make the rivers dry (severe drought conditions), and sell the land (the land shall be divided up, for the sake of its tremendous wealth) into the hand of the wicked (it shall become the possession of other nations): and I will make the land waste (the land shall be stripped of its abundance), and all that is therein (including its sons and its daughters), *by the hand of strangers* (by people of other nations): *I the Lord have spoken it* (It shall surely come to pass)." (Ezekiel 30:12). "When I shall make the land of Egypt desolate (dry, waste) and the country shall be destitute of that whereof it was full (the land shall be emptied of all its rich abundance), when I shall smite all them that dwell therein, then shall they know that I am the Lord."

History has borne out, over the many years, the fulfillment of this portion of prophecy in Africa. As aforementioned, the development of Africa's great wealth of natural and biological resources could not have been possible without European capital and technology. After all, an abundance of all the wealthy resources in the world means nothing at all if the Creator has stripped that nation's indigenous people of their ingenuities, abilities and know-how that it takes to develop their own resources. "And when I shall put thee out (extinguish thee), I will cover the heaven, and make the stars thereof dark: I will cover the sun with a cloud, and the moon shall not give her light." The explanation of this portion of scripture, taken from Ezekiel 32:7, is a little difficult to clarify lest one is willing to believe that God also uses the heavenly bodies to guide the course of the earth and its inhabitants. A section of Moses' instructions to the children of Israel in Deuteronomy 4:19 reads thus: "And lest thou lift up thine eyes unto heaven, and when thou seest the sun, and the moon, and the stars, even all the host of heaven, shouldest be driven to worship them, and serve them, *which the Lord thy God hath divided unto all nations under the whole heaven.*" God has ordained certain heavenly bodies that guide the course of all nations in the world, revealing creative knowledge to one or more persons of that nation, that can revolutionize it, giving it a uniqueness all its own. This is the creativeness of God that make us "different" nationalities with "different" types of creativity. Sometimes God creates a"star", someone He favors with a unique skill or ability that will benefit all of mankind, as a whole, yet he himself will stand out from all the rest, like a star, as did Imhotep, who was favored with an exceptional and wonderful mind. His accomplishments are a large part of the reason that the Ancient Egyptians stood out among the other nations during his time, and are still recognized as the greatest nation that ever was. Therefore, the stars, moon and the host of heaven "which the Lord our God hath divided unto *all nations* under the whole heaven" shall no longer impart its favors upon Egypt any longer, for ". . . all the bright lights of heaven will I make dark over thee, *and set darkness (ignorance) upon thy land,* saith the Lord God."

A quote from Ali A. Mazrui: "There is little doubt that in the modern period the black man has been scientifically marginal, in the sense of being left in the outer periphery of the scientific and technological achievement. And racists in Africa and elsewhere had pointed to the black man's scientific marginality as evidence that the black man was genetically less well endowed with mental and intellectual capabilities."

More than 85% of Africa's native people are yet quite primitive, having no perception of the value of their land and its resources, preferring to live on and work the land as farmers and fishermen. ". . . I shall . . . set darkness (ignorance) upon thy land."

" Africa's relative backwardness in technological capabilities made her vulnerable to the risk of having her resources depleted by others . . ." (A. Mazrui)

> "It came to pass also in the twelfth year, in the fifteenth day of the month that the word of the Lord came unto me saying, Son of man, wail for the multitude of Egypt, and cast them down, even her, and the daughters of the famous nations, unto the nether parts of the earth, with them that go down into the pit. Whom dost thou pass in beauty? Go down, and be thou laid with the uncircumcised. They shall fall in the midst of them that are slain by the sword: she is delivered to the sword: draw her and all her multitudes."—Ezekiel 32:17–20

It is only fourteen days later that the prophet Ezekiel receives this last and final word of warning for Pharaoh and all of Egypt, making a total of seven prophecies declared against the people and the land. The prophet is urged to 'wail for the multitude of Egypt', mourn deeply and sincerely, for they shall surely be cast down.

"Whom dost thou pass in beauty?" Again the prophet reminds them of this unusual and outstanding asset the Egyptians possessed: their very handsome facial features. Yet their physical beauty shall count for nothing, for it shall not save them from the very same fate as the nations gone before them. They shall not escape their fate. 'They shall fall in the midst of them that are slain by the sword.'

"The strong among the mighty shall speak to him out of the midst of hell with them that help him: they are gone down, they lie uncircumcised, slain by the sword. Asshur is there and all her company: his graves are about him: all of them slain, fallen by the sword: Whose graves are set in the sides of the pit, and her company is round about her grave: all of them slain, fallen by the sword, which caused terror in the land of the living. There is Elam and all her multitude round about her grave, all of them slain, fallen by the sword, which is gone down uncircumcised into the nether parts of the earth, which caused their terror in the land of the living; yet have they borne their shame with them that go down to the pit."—Ezekiel 32:21

God, the omniscient Deity who can 'see way down the road', had already taken a long look into the future of the nation of Egypt and saw that there would never be a day of repentance on the part of the Egyptians; never would there be a turning away from the worship of idols. And the prophet is instructed to foretell their destruction; however, it is not a destruction that is taken lightly. Knowing the sad consequences that shall accompany their downfall, the prophet must foretell it as one who has an affectionate concern, even love, for them; he must 'wail for the multitude of Egypt', even as he casts them down. However, the everloving God, in His mercy, attempts to appeal to the Egyptians even now by commanding the prophet to take Pharaoh through the very gates of hell and give him a 'preview' of the misery and sorrow that awaits them there. "The strong among the mighty shall speak to him out of the midst of hell with them that help him: they are gone down, they lie uncircumcised, slain by the sword."

Those who have already fallen are mentioned to the Pharaoh, the most recent being Asshur, the king of the nation of Assyria. "Asshur is there and all her company: his graves are about him: all of them slain. fallen by the sword." The great Assyrian empire and all the princes and mighty men of that monarchy, 'which caused terror in the land of the living', are now themselves 'slain, fallen by the sword.' There is Elam and all her multitude, which represented the kingdom of Persia and its numerous armies. The Elamites were a fierce and warlike people from the country known to the Greeks and Romans as Elymais, near Persia and Media. 'Yet have they borne their shame with them that go down to the pit . . .'

"They have set her a bed in the midst of the slain with all her multitude: her graves are round about him: all of them uncircumcised, slain by the sword: though their terror was caused in the land of the living, yet have they borne their shame with them that go down to the pit: he is put in the midst of them that be slain. There is Meshech, Tubal, and her multitude: her graves are round about him: all of them uncircumcised, slain by the sword, though they caused their terror in the land of the living. And they shall not lie with the mighty that are fallen of the uncircumcised, which are gone down to hell with their weapons of war: and they have laid their swords under their heads, but their iniquities shall be upon their bones, though they were the terror of the mighty in the land of the living. Yea, thou shalt be broken in the midst of the uncircumcised, and shalt lie with them that are slain with the sword."—Ezekiel 32:25–28

'There is Meshech, Tubal, and all her multitude . . . slain by the sword, though they (too) caused their terror in the land of the living.' These represented the Scythian powers, a fierce, barbarous group of tribes of the northern nations, who had often been troublesome to the Assyrians and other nations. Their latest descent upon the Medes, which lasted for some years, had finally ended in a bloody defeat under Cyaxares, king of the Medes.

The glory of a warrior's burial was the custom of burying them with their swords, shields and helmets under their heads. '. . . they have laid their sword under their heads . . .' However, the pomp and ceremony of this ancient custom would not keep their sins from following them into the judgement, '. . . but their iniquities shall be upon their bones . . .' All these facts were delivered to Pharaoh as a final warning to him and to Egypt, yet the prophet knows that the warning will go unheeded: '. . . Yea, thou shalt be broken . . . and shalt lie with them . . .'

> "There is Edom, her kings and all her princes, which with their might are laid by them that were slain by the sword: they shall lie with the uncircumcised, and with them that go down to the pit. There be the princes of the north, all of them, and all the Zidonians, which are gone down with the slain; with their terror they are ashamed of their might; and they lie uncircumcised with them that be slain by the sword and bear their shame with them that go down to the pit."—Ezekiel 32:29–30

The kingdom of Edom had flourished a long time, although not near as long as Egypt, because the Edomites were the descendants of Esau, Isaac's oldest son. Her king and all her princes, mentioned in 1 Chronicles 1:43–54, were also 'slain by the sword'. Even the Zidonians, who were as well acquainted with maritime affairs as the Egyptians, were 'gone down with the slain'.

The prophet stresses that these six nations, Asshur, Elam, Meshech, Tubal, Edom and Zidon, have been shorned of their might and power and have been delivered over to death and hell. This prominent display of their destructions was to emphasize the fact that they too boasted great power and great might; yet they, who were the wisest, wealthiest and strongest of their neighbors, have now been laid waste, 'slain by the sword'. In view of the many persistent warnings from the Lord, it is clear that Pharaoh and Egypt need not have perished with the other nations. However, the prophet's pleading is of no avail, for the Lord God further instructs the prophet with these final words:

> "Pharaoh shall see them, and shall be comforted over all his multitude, even Pharaoh and all his army slain by the sword, saith the Lord God. For I have caused my terror in the land of the living: and he shall be laid in the midst of the uncircumcised with them that are slain with the sword *even Pharaoh and all his multitude, saith the Lord God.*"—Ezekiel 32:31

"It is futile", says the Lord God "to continue these warnings". In spite of all the prophesying and pleading to Pharaoh, and even

185

going so far as to point out to him the downfall of his neighboring nations who were also the 'terror of the mighty in the land of the living'—these shall avail nothing. "Pharaoh shall see them . . .", meaning Egypt shall not escape, but shall suffer the same fate and shall soon join them. "For I have caused My *terror* in the land of the living . . ." In other words, 'They have had their day now I shall have mine. I have already set in motion even right now the laws of this prophecy and have commenced destruction upon Egypt. ". . . he shall be laid in the midst . . . with them that are slain with the sword, *even Pharaoh and all his multitude, saith the Lord God.*"

Conclusion

The prophets—Isaiah, Jeremiah and Ezekiel—were allowed by God to supernaturally gaze into the future of the Egyptians, spanning the time from the beginning of the prophecy, through the centuries, to its fulfillment. Although Ezekiel's account is not written in perfect chronological order, it is generally believed that the 30th chapter represents the account of the very last prophecy that was delivered to Pharaoh. Ezekiel, who was the very last prophet to appear before Pharaoh, was approached by God at least seven different times over a period of fifteen to seventeen years with warnings and pleadings to Pharaoh and Egypt of His pending judgement. The fulfillment of these judgements against the Eyptians are fully documented in the pages of history.

Ezekiel Chapter 29

God declares that He is "against Pharaoh, king of Egypt . . . which hath said, My river is mine own, and *I have made it for myself.*" In addition to their sin of sorcery and idolatry, Pharaoh adds to it pride and conceit. The Lord determines: ". . . I will bring thee up out of the midst of *thy rivers* . . ." The bountiful plenty and prosperity afforded the Egyptians by the Nile River shall cease for they shall be removed from their famous well known habitation on the Nile and it shall no more be the center of their overweening pride and boasting. ". . . I will leave thee thrown into the wilderness, thee and all the fish of *thy rivers.*" The reference to the 'wilderness' means the 'bush', or 'rain forest', a familiar environmental condition associated with the continent of Africa. Some historians believe that the Yoruba people of the West African coastal area surrounding Benin City in present-day Nigeria *migrated direct from the Nile to the Niger*, taking with them the techniques of working in bronze.

187

They shall be scattered all over the jungles in various places, ". . . *thou shalt fall upon the 'open fields' . . .*" The purpose of the scattering was to prevent their ever coming together as a people again, ". . . *thou shalt not be brought together, nor gathered . . .*"

Moreover, there would always be a dominating fear of being attacked by wild animals: ". . . *I have given thee for meat to the beasts of the field and to the fowls of the heaven.*" Also drought and famine shall prevail in the land: "And the land of Egypt shall be desolate and waste . . . *because* he hath said. 'The river is mine, and I have made it. Behold, therefore I am against thee, and *against thy rivers, and I will make the land of Egypt utterly waste and desolate, from the tower of Syene even unto the border of Ethiopia.*" The drought, famine and desert conditions of the continent is the fulfillment of this prophecy.

Egypt was never to be the same again. As Egyptian culture began to gradually disintegrate, the Egyptians tended to rely on mercenaries from Nubia, Sudan, Canaan, Sardinia, Libya and other places to fight in their armies. As a result, foreigners rose to high positions in the state while Egyptians turned more and more to the sedate professions of priest or scribe which could be passed on to their sons. Consequently, Egyptian society stagnated. Meanwhile, Philistines took over mastery of the seas. Unemployment among Egyptian mercenaries increased as well as lawlessness and dishonesty among officials. And to make bad matters worse, there were famines caused by low tides of the Nile, causing violence among people desperate with hunger and a waning in the worship of the Pharaoh as a god.

Egypt shall no longer be elevated above the nations: "It shall be the *basest* of the kingdoms; neither shall it *exalt* itself any more above the nations: *for I shall diminish them*, that they shall no more rule over the nations." Considering the progress the Egyptians had already made in the various fields of technology, there is no doubt that had they been allowed to continue at the same rate of progress, this world would be further advanced in every field of endeavor that man can imagine!

188

"*And I . . . will sell the land into the hand of the wicked: and I will make the land waste, and all that is therein, by the hand of strangers; I the Lord have spoken it.*" Mazrui states: "Asia's attractiveness was initially as a market; Africa's attractiveness when it came was initially as a source of natural and human resources. The products needed from Africa over the centuries ranged from slaves to uranium, from peanuts to diamonds. The copper and gold, the diamonds and the agricultural products served the appetites of others abroad. Africa might indeed have been impoverished by much of the resource exploitation which went on . . ." '. . . *and the country shall be destitute of that whereof it was full . . .*' The resources present in the continent today have been there all the time, through the centuries, because God, who is omniscient, knew that in the ensuing centuries such resources as uranium, copper, oil, phosphates and gas—resources not required in the era of the ancient Pharaohs—would certainly be in great demand in these times. Consider the fact that the one important mineral not discovered in Africa before 1945 was *petroleum*. In that year an American oil company secured petroleum rights in Ethiopia.

The fact that this wealth exists in such great abundance in the continent of Africa, as nowhere else in the world, is certainly an indication that the great and wonderful plan of world leadership that God had purposed from the beginning for the Egyptians and their descendants was intended to be colossal, to say the least! However, this divine plan came to a perfect end when God Almighty declared: ". . . neither shall it (Egypt) exalt itself any more *above the nations: for I will diminish them*, that they shall no more *rule over the nations.*" In view of this astounding fact, it's certainly safe to say that if the Ancient Egyptians had been allowed to continue to dominate and influence the world scene, what with their wealth of natural resources and outstanding knowledge and abilities, there is no doubt that the black man would be ruling the world today. But alas! their sin and disobedience moved God to declare: "... and there shall be no more a prince (Pharaoh) of the land of Egypt..." The ruling scepter, and all that pertains to it, shall be totally removed. All of Egypt's great might and power was completely diminished when God also declared, "... I have broken the arm of Pharaoh king of Egypt; and lo, it shall not be bound up to be healed (shall never recover their original strength), to put a roller to bind it, to make it strong to hold the sword (neither shall there be any remedy that will restore it). He determines to withdraw His power and strength from the Egyptians and bestow it upon the king of Babylon, Nebuchadnezzar: "But I will strengthen the arms of the king of Babylon ... when I shall put my sword into the hand of the king of Babylon ..." The entrance of the reign of Nebuchadnezzar marked the end of Egyptian rule. Fourteen years earlier, in the approximate year of 603 B.C., God had already appeared to Nebuchadnezzar in a dream and shown him that his kingdom would be exalted above the other kingdoms. In the dream he was shown an image "whose head was of fine gold, his breast and his arms of silver, his belly and his thighs of brass." The dream, found in the second chapter of the book of Daniel, was interpreted to Nebuchadnezzar by the prophet Daniel: "Thou, O king, art a king of kings: for the God of heaven hath given thee a kingdom, power and strength, and glory. And wheresoever the children of men dwell, the beasts of the field and the fowls of the heaven hath he given into thine hand, and hath made thee ruler over them all. Thou art this head of gold." Nebuchadnezzar's kingdom was to be the last of the 'great' kingdoms—"And after thee shall arise another kingdom inferior to thee"—closing out the "Golden Era" of the truly great and powerful kingdoms. Every succeeding kingdom thereafter could not compare to their greatness, wealth and power.

"And I will scatter the Egyptians among the nations, and disperse them among the countries; and they shall know that I am the Lord." It is erroneously presumed among many nations today that all dark-skinned peoples are automatically of African-Egyptian descent. However, this is not the case. It must be understood that during the era of the Egyptians there were also other nations of the ancient world who were dark-skinned people. According to archaeological findings, it is now an established fact that the first ancient civilizations in the beginning, were indeed black. Asia's lower Mesopotamian indigenous population (the Sumerians) were black. The nations of Arabia, India, Phoenicia, Crete, Canaan, and portions of Persia, just to name a few, were also dark-skinned people. However, when the Bible makes mention of the people of 'The Land of Egypt', it is in reference to the people that occupied the continent of Africa, including Ethiopia, sometimes referred to as 'Cush' and Nubia, known for their famous men called Nubians. Sheba and others that dwelt within the continent, including Libya. History relates that in early times all of North Africa above the Sahara was known as Libya. The ancient writers used the name 'Libya' to refer to the entire continent of Africa even as late as the 17th century. It was used as an alternate name for the entire continent. Our current Bibles that display a map of the nations of the ancient worlds, will often refer to Egypt as 'Libya'. True, these other nations were dark in color, as were the Egyptians, but they were not 'culturally linked' with the Egyptians. It was the uniqueness of the Egyptians' culture that made them truly Egyptian, a culture not based on blackness of skin, which in that time was basically very common, but a culture bred out of notable deeds based in outstanding, God-given ingenuity that simply did not exist among the other dark-skinned nations. The unique singularity of their remarkable abilities and possessions was actually the foundation of their culture, a peculiarity that made them stand alone, above the nations. The northern area of Africa bordering the Mediterranean Sea had been in touch with Europe from earliest times. Yet, the great Egyptian civilization, as we know it, was not a transplant from Europe or the Middle East but was a unique culture that developed on African soil. Put simply, the Egyptians were God's specially-chosen people of that time, a choice that was made by God Himself, long before the nation of Israel even came into existence.

The Arabs that occupy present-day Egypt are often mistakenly thought of as the lineal descendants of the Ancient Egyptians. Nothing could be further from the truth. As a matter of fact, there are two basic reasons why the Arabs of Northern Africa are not the direct lineal descendants of the Ancient Egyptians: (1) The Arabs descended upon the continent of Africa in 639 A.D. when general Amru ibn-al-as invaded North Africa, bringing their way of life and their religion into Africa, with virtually all of the Egyptians, except the Christian Copts, embracing Mohammedanism. The Arabs were simply one of the many nations whom God had prophesied would invade the land. ". . . *I will therefore spread out my net over thee with a company of many people* . . ." However, of all the foreign settlements in Africa, the Arabs made the greatest impact. The Islamic religion spread from North Africa to areas of the Sahara so that many of the African peoples as the Hausa, Kanuri, Songhai, and the Mandingo are largely Islamized. Soon the Arabs were completely absorbed into the rest of the population. Today it is hard to distinguish one whose ancestors were Arabs from one whose forbears were the original inhabitants. The advent of the Arabs, along with all the other nations that invaded Africa, was a part of the fulfillment of the prophecy by Ezekiel ". . . *the terrible of the nations, all of them* . . ." (Ezekiel 32:12).

(2) The second reason is that the history of the Arabs have not followed the conditions of the prophecy that was pronounced against the Ancient Egyptians. The fulfillment of the prophecy does not apply to any portion of the history of the Arabs. The Arab nation does not have a history of slavery and captivity. They have never existed in the jungles; as a matter of fact, Northern Africa has a very different culture from the lands below the Sahara

192

Desert. And they are certainly not considered the 'basest of the kingdoms'. Frankly speaking, just the opposite is true. Their lives have followed the prophecy given to Abraham concerning his son Ishmael: "And as for Ishmael, I have heard thee: Behold, I have *blessed* him, and will make him *fruitful*, and will *multiply him exceedingly*, twelve princes shall he beget, and I will *make him a great nation.*" (Genesis 17:20). On the other hand, history has revealed that the lives of black people of African descent have followed every portion of the prophecy levied against the Ancient Egyptians, throughout the centuries, line upon line, precept upon precept, even to this very day proving them to be the direct lineal descendants of the Ancient Egyptians!

As forestated, the Arab nation is simply one of the nations that have settled, of late, on the continent of Africa, enjoying along with the other foreign nations, the bounty that is to be found in the northern section of Africa.

"And I will scatter the Egyptians among the nations, and disperse them among the countries; and they shall know that I am the Lord." Although Egyptian descendants have been scattered far and wide, all over the world, yet the influence of' Egyptian civilization upon black Africa and its descendants may be seen at many levels. Linguists have found relationships between the Egyptian and the Bantu languages. "The most fascinating proofs of ancient links between Africa's widely spread peoples are the Sudanic kingdoms. Although these have existed as far away as West Africa and the Transvaal, their institutions are so strikingly similar that they must have developed from a common source. *That source is certainly Ancient Egypt.* The core of these societies was the divine power of the ruler, who acted as the intermediary between his people and the supernatural.

The similarity with the religious forms of Egypt in the time of the Pharaohs must be accepted as more than coincidence. It is believed that the influence traveled through Cush to the communities along the southern rim of the Sahara at least 1,500 years ago." (Discovery of Africa).

193

The persistent, reiterating phrase, ". . . *and they shall know that I am the Lord* . . ." indicates God's sole purpose—that when the fulfillment of these prophecies shall have come to pass, then they shall know who is the true God. ". . . they shall know that I am the Lord", because there is no other god who, after declaring the fate of an entire nation, is also able to bring it to pass—no other god but the true God, Jehovah, the Omnipotent.

Ezekiel Chapter 31

It is this particular chapter that emphasizes and points out the universal greatness and power of the Egyptians and the uniqueness of their unparalleled handsome facial features. The prophet is instructed to address Egypt's unequalled greatness first. ". . . Son of man, speak to Pharaoh, king of Egypt, and to his multitude; *whom art thou like in thy greatness?*" More is known, with certainty, of Ancient Egyptian activities than of any other ancient civilization. Scholars have been attracted to the study of Egyptian antiquities since the 16th century. Scientific expeditions have been sent to Egypt since 1798. The climate is extraordinarily dry, rain falling only about once in five years, and as a result, the soil is rather dry and easily removeable. The ancient relics and monuments, therefore, have resisted decomposition for thousands of years, and have been dug out of the sand with relative ease. The Egyptians placed all manner of objects in their elaborate tombs, objects that furnished a detailed continous record of their daily existence. The walls of the tombs speak volumes of the greatness of the nation. From about 1500 to 1200 B.C. Egypt, as the richest and for a long time the most successful power in Biblical Africa, was a major recipient of slaves. It was the first great age of slavery. It was the Egyptians' custom to turn prisoners of war, if they were not slaughtered on the spot, into conscript soldiers. *"To whom art thou thus like in glory and in greatness among the trees of Eden? Yet shalt thou be brought down with the trees of Eden unto the nether parts of the earth* . . . this is Pharoah and all his multitude, saith the Lord God."

"*The cedars in the garden of God could not hide him . . . nor any tree in the garden of God was like unto him in his beauty.*" In the words of Matthew Henry: "He (the Egyptian) was comely with the comeliness that God had placed upon him. For He that gave them their beauty, if they be deprived of it, knows how to turn it into deformity." The extraordinary handsomeness of the Egyptians was a trademark commonly known and recognized, a phenomenon not customarily found among the other dark-skinned nations. The loss of it is also a trademark commonly known and recognized among Egyptian descendants, a phenomenon not customarily found among the other dark-skinned nations, as the people of India and others. The unique handsomeness that the ancient Egyptians possessed has once again begun to surface commonly among Black people of African descent. A beauty not dependent upon the presence of other ethnic strains in the heritage, but the emergence of that uniqueness of beauty that only the Egyptians possessed.

"*And I will scatter the Egyptians among the nations, and will disperse them through the countries. Yet, thus saith the Lord; at the end of forty years will I gather the Egyptians from the people whither they were scattered: . . . and they shall be there a base kingdom.*" This first

King Tutankhamen—an example of the classic ancient beauty of the Egyptians.

scattering of the Egyptians, over a period of forty years, more or less, was obviously intended to dissolve the culture and the lifestyle of the Egyptians, making it impossible for them to reestablish Egyptian society as it formerly was. The textual translation of the number 'forty years' is a bit obscure, not readily understood, therefore, it is not clear exactly how many actual years the Egyptians were scattered before they were again gathered back into the land of Pathros (sub-Sahara), which would be the land of their habitation. However, God has declared that when they are brought together again as a kingdom 'they shall be *there* a base kingdom.'

". . . *neither shall it exalt itself any more above the nations* . . ." After this proclamation, no Egyptian kingdom that attempted to attain and sustain great power was ever successful. Beginning about the eighth century three powerful black states—Mali, Songhay and Ghana—began to emerge in the western Sudan, a broad open country located between the Sahara in the north and the Guinea Coast on the south. Their power and wealth were based on trade with caravans loaded with fruit, salt, sugar, clothing, wheat and other products that were exchanged for gold. It is said that Ghana controlled trade in the Sudan and ruled there for almost 300 years. It is also said that the rulers of Ghana were fabulously rich and was one of the main suppliers of gold for North Africa and Europe.

After Ghana fell, Mali rose in the 13th century and became a great empire. Mali declined in the fifteenth century and was replaced by Songhay. Of the three empires, Songhay was the most prosperous. It's greatest city, popularly known as Timbuktu, was the intellectual center of this black empire, famous for its scholars and its social life. According to an excerpt from *Before the Mayflower*: "Youths from all over the Moslem world came to Timbuktu to study law and surgery at the University of Sankore; scholars came from North Africa and Europe to confer with the learned historians and writers of the black empire. Es Sadi, a Timbuktu intellectual who wrote a history of the Sudan, said his brother came from Jenne for a successful cataract operation at the hands of a distinguished surgeon."

197

'In Timbuktu', Leo Africanus said, 'there are numerous judges, doctors, and clerics, all receiving good salaries from the king. He pays great respect to men of learning . . .'

Leo Africanus, a Christanized Moor who visited the city in the sixteenth century, said "it is a wonder to see what plenty of merchandise is daily brought hither and how costly and sumptuous all things be . . . Here are many shops of . . . merchants and especially of such as weave linen."

The great city of Timbuktu, with its fine university and other intellectual centers; its judges, doctors, surgeons, clerics, rich merchants and fine linen weaving, finally declined in the 17th century, bringing to an end the reign of these three great African empires. Question: Why did these empires collapse? An interesting note from *The Mayflower*: "Es-Sadi, who wrote the *Tarikh Al-Sudan* in the dying days of the Songhay empire 'At this moment', he said, 'faith was exchanged for infidelity; there was nothing forbidden by God which was not openly done . . . Because of these abominations, the Almighty in his vengeance drew upon the Songhai the victorious army of the Moors.'" These great black states could not maintain their empires for the long period of time that their ancestors, the Ancient Egyptians had—proving beyond a shadow of doubt that it was God who established the original Ancient Egyptian civilization, developed it, and maintained it. Therefore, it was impossible for these empires—Mali, Ghana and Songhay—to exist for very long without Almighty God to sustain them. *"They shall no more rule over the nations."*

The Mayflower states: "The age of the great Sudan empires ended, but several states to the east and south, notably Mossi, Hausa, Kanem-Bornu and Ashanti, retained political identities down to the eighteenth and nineteenth centuries. Great Zimbabwe and other stone cities in Southern Africa suggest that strong states flourished inland. Vigorous centers of culture also existed on the East Coast, where Black and Arab merchants traded with India and China."

After these empires lost their importance in controlling the main external markets, Africa began to be exploited. Thus began the slave trades to the Americas and to the East; the discovery and exploitation of minerals and of profitable export crops, ending with the dividing up of the continent among the nations, with Great Britain controlling an area more than 40 times as large as the British Isles. *"Thus saith the Lord God; I will therefore spread out my net over thee with a company of many people; and they shall bring thee up in my net."*

"And when I shall put thee out (extinguish thee, put out your bright lights) . . . all the bright lights of heaven will I make dark over thee, and set darkness (ignorance) upon thy land . . ." All things are done through the wisdom of Almighty God. In Proverbs the eighth chapter, the wisdom of God speaks as if it were an individual person in its own right: "The Lord possessed me in the beginning of his way, before his works of old. I was set up from everlasting, from the beginning, or ever the earth was . . . *I wisdom dwell with prudence* (skill and good judgement in the use of resources) *and find out knowledge of witty inventions* (creative abilities). The extraordinary ingenuity of the Egyptian people was the awesome wisdom of God Himself. The creative ability required to build the famous pyramids, plus the uncommon intelligence of the Egyptians whose wisdom was sought after by their own fellow neighbors, were all governed by God's wisdom because wisdom, in the fullest sense, belongs to God alone. Therefore when God ordained, "I will cover the heaven, and make the stars thereof dark; I will cover the sun . . . and the moon shall not give her light . . . All the bright lights of heaven will I make dark over thee . . .", this was really bad news for the Egyptians. In other words, His fountain of wisdom and knowledge shall be closed and no more shall the knowledge of witty inventions be inspired to them, nor shall creative abilities pour forth upon the ungrateful Egyptians. He thereafter determined to set darkness (ignorance) upon their land.

It is for this reason that Africa's scientific and technological achievements have been nonexistent. An interesting article from the book *Africa's International Relations*, by Ali A. Mazrui states: "It was not simply the lack of the written word that delayed scientific flowering in Africa; it was also the lack of the written *numeral*. Jack Goody has drawn attention to the relationship between writing and mathematics, and the implications of the absence of both in some African societies. The absence of mathematics at the more elaborate level was bound to hamper considerably black Africa's scientific development." All the bright lights of heaven will I make dark over thee, *and set darkness (ignorance) upon thy land.*"

"*I will also vex the hearts of many people, when I shall bring thy destruction among the nations, into the countries which thou hast not known.*" The hatred of 'many people' for the Black man was in fulfillment of the prophesy of God, 'I wlll also *vex* the hearts of *many people.*' However, bear in mind that, as forestated, the prophesy has been fulfilled because the Saviour, Jesus Christ and the Great One Martin Luther King, have come, bringing it to an end, as the Lord God promised. This truth is evident when we observe the favor that God has placed in the hearts of 'many people' towards the black man in recent years. Many Blacks have obtained great popularity and prosperity; moreover, in Africa, Kenya for instance, plantations have been given back to African farmers. The government bought plantations from British farmers, divided up the land into small plots and distributed them to the African farmers.

"*When I shall make the land of Egypt desolate, and the country shall be destitute of that whereof it was full . . .*" Although Africa has been 'destituted of that whereof it was full' for the past three centuries, developments within the country, however, have changed tremendously. As a matter fact, by the early 1950s African independence movements were widespread, marking the beginning of the rapid decline of imperial powers in Africa. Following two disastrous world wars, Western Europe no longer had the military or economlc capacity to continue its imperialism. Reinforcing this situation was the shift in the world balance of power with the rise of the Soviet

Union and the United States as the dominant powers of the latter 20th century. Just as God stepped in centuries ago effecting changes on the world scene that commenced the beginning of the prophecy against the Egyptians, He also stepped in to effect changes to bring to pass its ending, as well. As a result, black Africans became increasingly aware of their own potential power, an awareness that began to manifest itself in effective actions toward emancipation. Although the inevitable transition from colonial rule to self-rule became bloody and rough in many places, it was also relatively peaceful in others. By 1980, fifty-one African states had acquired their sovereignty, ending with Zimbabwe, the last major colonial territory, and the White minority was forced to share power with the black majority. However, it is this very fact that accounts for the continued conflict between South African authorities and black nationalist groups in South Africa. The South African white government has maintained a policy of apartheid (meaning "apartness") which maintains separation and separate development of the races. Some countries feel that the Republic of South Africa is too rich and self-sustaining to be forced, through external pressure, into even modifying their racial policies, much less to completely relinquish their power altogether. This situation, however, shall not last because it was God who ordained the reign of the whites in the first place to serve His purpose and it is God who has ordained that their reign must now end. "And the Lord shall smite Egypt: *He shall smite and heal it.*"

The word 'heal' does not mean 'restore' because the Egyptians (Africans), as a nation and as a people, shall not regain the prominence and eminence that was once the proud possession of their ancestors. The greatness bestowed upon the Ancient Egyptians was given because they were a special people whom God had chosen to bless with His divine favor. This 'special favor', however, was lost through disobedience and was bestowed upon the Jews, a fact related to them by the prophet Isaiah: "For I am the Lord thy God, the Holy One of Israel, thy Saviour: *I gave Egypt for thy ransom,*

201

Ethiopia and Seba (Sheba) for thee." (Isaiah 43:3). Egypt shall be 'healed' but shall never again, in this lifetime, be restored back to the glory of its first estate of power, honor and wealth. This special grace that was bestowed upon Egypt of old shall never again be restored in the same way as before but must now be obtained by those who choose to obtain it through God's Son, *Jesus, the Messiah*. It is these special Egyptian descendants who choose to accept God's Son as their Saviour, in this lifetime, that shall enjoy the blessings of the Lord in that eternal day, and shall be restored once again as a great nation: "And it shall come to pass *in that day*, that the Lord shall set his hand again the *second time* to recover the remnant of his people, which shall be left, from Assyria, *and from Egypt, and from Pathros, and from Cush*, and from Elam, and from Shinar, and from Hamath, and from the islands of the sea. And he shall set up an ensign (flag) for the nations . . ." (Isaiah 11:11–12). "*In that day* shall Israel be the third with *Egypt* and with Assyria, even a blessing in the midst of the land. Whom the Lord of hosts shall bless, saying, *blessed be Egypt my people*, and Assyria the work of my hands, and Israel mine inheritance." (Isaiah 19:24–25).

Obviously, there are many who are faithful to believe that in time, Africa shall once again regain her greatness in this lifetime, and find it offensive that anyone could be so positive that this shall never be. However, there is a phenomenon that even now hinders the progress of Africa and that phenomenon is Africa's almost unanimous break wlth Israel in 1973. This action was most unwise. God promised Abraham: "And I will *bless* them that *bless* thee, and *curse* him that *curseth* thee: and in thee shall all families of the earth be blessed."

Bear in mind that Egypt's downfall did not occur overnight, but over a period of time. Nevertheless, it did come—a fact that the United States, which is the most prosperous nation in the entire world, should t̨ake into consideration. Because of sin, the United States even now teeters on the borderline of God's judgement, a judgement already begun with the United Nations seating of the People's Republic of China in 1971 and the rise of Arab power from 1973 until now. These two seemingly unimportant events marked the end of American domination in the United Nations and the end of America's role as a decisive force in the World Body. Only God knows whether that power shall ever be restored.

Take into consideration a statement taken from the book *Africa's International Relations*, written by Ali A. Mazrui, describing what he calls *Counter-Penetration*: "Until now, the Third World has been penetrated by the developed world (Britain, France, USA) culturally, economically and politically. The question which now arises is whether it is possible for some of the new resources of Third World countries to be used for *Counter-Penetration* into the major citadels of the economic powers in Western Europe and *North America*. Such *Counter-Penetration* into western economies should to some extent make them as vulnerable to pressure from the Third World. Some Third World intellectuals say the answer is *disengagement*. They urge, 'Let us move in the dlrection of disengagement, let us cut loose from the international capitalist system, let us assert our own autonomy'. Disengagement as a strategy would probably be less effective than the strategy of *Counter-Penetration*. Imagine Saudi Arabia disengaged from the international capitalist system. Where would Saudi Arabia's economic power be in such a move? . . . To *sell oil, to get people to need its oil, to get the mighty to be dependent on it— that is an act of Counter-Penetration.*

The *oil-rich third world countries* should indeed use some of their dollar reserves to buy shares in major multi-national companies in the West. They should invest in new industrial ventures, *buy out the major powers themselves in their own companies, give loans to major industrial countries,* and increase the vulnerability of the *northern hemisphere* to effective lobbying by the underprivileged Southern Hemisphere."

No nation, regardless of power or prosperity, can even hope to maintain its greatness without the presence of Almighty God, who determines whether they shall stand or whether they shall fall.

The glorious Egyptian past of the African black man, hidden, buried and forgotten for so long, shall become known in the days ahead, simply because it is God's chosen time that it become known. Many shall believe, a few will not—nevertheless, the prophecy is fulfilled. Those who do not believe will remain in the jungles or 'down on the plantation'. But those who choose to believe will, in the days ahead, walk in a new freedom such as the modern-day black man has not experienced since the days of the Egyptians. Hopefully, we shall be wiser in our time than our ancestors—*The Ancient Egyptians*.

Bibliography

Allen, William D. and Jerry E. Jennings. *Man in Africa.* Edited by Benjamin E. Thomas. Grand Rapids, Michigan: The Fiedler Company, 1974.

Barker, William P. *Everyone in the Bible.* Westwood, New Jersey: Fleming H. Revell Company, 1966.

Barnes, Albert. *Notes on the Old and New Testament.* Edited by Robert Frew, D.D. Grand Rapids, Michigan: Baker Book House, 1980.

Bennett, Lerone Jr. *Before the Mayflower-A History of Black America.* Chicago, Illinois: Johnson Publishing Company, Inc., 1987.

Carter, Leroy H. *Black Heroes of the Bible.* Columbus, Georgia: Brentwood Christian Press, 1989.

Cruden, Alexander. *Cruden's Complete Concordance.* Eds. A. D. Adams, C.H. Irwin, S.A. Waters. Grand Rapids, Michigan: Zondervan Publishing House, 1968.

Hall, Richard. *Discovery of Africa.* New York: Grosset & Dunlap, 1970.

Johnson, Paul. *The Civilization of Ancient Egypt.* New York: Atheneum, 1978.

Lockyer, Herbert. *All the Kings and Queens of the Bible.* Grand Rapids, Michigan: Zondervan Publishing House, 1961.

Mazrui, Ali. A. *The African Series.* PMI Films. 5547 N. Ravenswood, Chicago, Illinois.

McCray, Walter Arthur. *The Black Presence in the Bible*. Chicago, Illinois: Black Light Fellowship, 1989.

Smith, William. *The New Smith's Bible Dictionary*. Edited by Reuel G. Lemmons. Garden City, New York: Doubleday & Company, Inc.

Vine, W.E. *Vine's Expository Dictionary of Old and New Testament Words*. Edited by F.F. Bruce. Iowa Falls, Iowa: World Bible Publishers, 1981.

Encyclopedia Britannica-1986 Book of the Year. 1986 ed.

Lands and Peoples. New York: Grolier Incorporated, 1965.

Matthew Henry's Commentary on the Whole Bible. New York: Fleming H. Revell Company, 1951.

The Book of Knowledge-The Children's Encyclopedia. New York: Grolier Incorporated, 1965.

The New Encyclopedia Britannica. 1983 ed.

The New Funk & Wagnalls Encyclopedia. New York: Unicorn Publishing, Inc., 1953.

The World Almanac and Book of Facts. 1989 ed.

The World Book Encyclopedia. Chicago: Field Enterprises, Inc., 1955.

Universal Standard Encyclopedia. New York: Standard Reference Works Publishing Company, Inc., 1956.